KU-519-516

Decision Mathematics 2

Stan Dolan

Series editor Hugh Neill

CAMBRIDGE
UNIVERSITY PRESS

CAMBRIDGE UNIVERSITY PRESS
Cambridge, New York, Melbourne, Madrid, Cape Town, Singapore, São Paulo, Delhi

Cambridge University Press
The Edinburgh Building, Cambridge CB2 8RU, UK

www.cambridge.org
Information on this title: www.cambridge.org/9780521619158

© Cambridge University Press 2001, 2005

This publication is in copyright. Subject to statutory exception
and to the provisions of relevant collective licensing agreements,
no reproduction of any part may take place without the written
permission of Cambridge University Press.

First published as *Discrete Mathematics 2* 2001
Second edition 2005
Reprinted 2007, 2009

Printed in the United Kingdom at the University Press, Cambridge

A catalogue record for this publication is available from the British Library

ISBN 978-0-521-61915-8 paperback

Cambridge University Press has no responsibility for the persistence or
accuracy of URLs for external or third-party Internet websites referred to in
this publication, and does not guarantee that any content on such websites is,
or will remain, accurate or appropriate. Information regarding prices, travel
timetables and other factual information given in this work are correct at
the time of first printing but Cambridge University Press does not guarantee
the accuracy of such information thereafter.

Cover image © Digital Vision

Please note that the following AQA (AEB) and AQA (NEAB) questions used (pp. 35, 36, 53,
54, 55, 56, 73, 74) are *not* from the live examinations for the current specification.

Contents

Introduction

Cambridge Advanced Level Mathematics has been written especially for the OCR Mathematics specification. It consists of one book or half-book corresponding to each module. This book is the second Decision Mathematics module, D2.

The books are divided into chapters roughly corresponding to specification headings. Occasionally a section includes an important result that is difficult to prove or outside the specification. These sections are marked with an asterisk (*) in the section heading, and there is usually a sentence early on explaining precisely what it is that the student needs to know.

It is important to recognise that, while every effort has been made by the author and by OCR to make the books match the specification, the books do not and must not define the examination. It is conceivable that questions might be asked in the examination, examples of which do not appear specifically in the books.

Occasionally within the text paragraphs appear in a grey box. These paragraphs are usually outside the main stream of the mathematical argument, but may help to give insight, or suggest extra work or different approaches.

Numerical work is presented in a form intended to discourage premature approximation. In ongoing calculations inexact numbers appear in decimal form like 3.456... , signifying that the number is held in a calculator to more places than are given. Numbers are not rounded at this stage; the full display could be either 3.456 123 or 3.456 789. Final answers are then stated with some indication that they are approximate, for example '1.23 correct to 3 significant figures'.

There are plenty of exercises, and each chapter contains a Miscellaneous exercise which includes examination questions. Most of these questions were set in OCR examinations; some were set in AQA examinations. Questions which go beyond examination requirements are marked by an asterisk. At the end of the book there are a set of Revision exercises and two practice examination papers. The author thanks Jan Dangerfield who contributed to these exercises, and who also read the book very carefully and made many extremely useful and constructive comments.

AQA(AEB) and AQA(NEAB) examination questions are reproduced by permission of the Assessment and Qualifications Alliance.

The author thanks OCR and Cambridge University Press for their help in producing this book. However, the responsibility for the text, and for any errors, remains with the author.

1 Matching

This chapter is about matching the elements of one set with elements of another. When you have completed it you should

- be able to represent a matching problem by means of a bipartite graph
- be able to find a maximal matching
- be able to apply the Matching Augmentation algorithm
- be able to interpret allocation problems as matching problems where cost must be minimised
- know how to use the Hungarian algorithm to solve allocation problems.

1.1 Introduction

Matching the elements of two different sets is a common task which you often perform without being aware of it. When you distribute copies of a newsletter to your friends you are matching the set of newsletters with the set of friends. In this case the task is easy because any copy can be assigned to any friend.

Matching becomes more difficult when the two sets to be matched have characteristics that make certain assignments undesirable or impossible. For example, in matching people with jobs, the skills of the people and the requirements of the jobs mean that some assignments should not be made.

Bipartite graphs provide a useful way to represent such **matching problems**. You met the idea of a bipartite graph in D1 Section 2.1.

> A **bipartite graph** is a graph with two sets of nodes such that arcs only connect nodes from one set to the other and do not connect nodes within a set.

It is convenient to always consider the two sets of nodes of a bipartite graph to be the **left-nodes** and the **right-nodes**. For example, $K_{3,3}$ would be drawn as shown in Fig. 1.1.

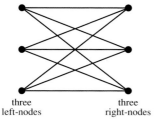

three
left-nodes

three
right-nodes

Fig. 1.1

The two sets of nodes correspond to the two sets to be matched and the arcs correspond to the assignments that can be made.

> For any bipartite graph, a **matching** is a set of arcs which have no nodes in common.
>
> A **maximal matching** is any matching which contains the largest possible number of arcs.

You have already met a matching problem in D1 Exercise 2A Question 8. Example 1.1.1 shows the problem again.

Example 1.1.1

Four Members of Parliament, Ann, Brian, Clare and David, are being considered for four cabinet posts. Ann could be Foreign Secretary or Home Secretary, Brian could be Home Secretary or the Chancellor of the Exchequer, Clare could be Foreign Secretary or the Minister for Education and David could be the Chancellor or the Home Secretary.

(a) Draw a bipartite graph to represent this situation.

(b) How many options does the Prime Minister have?

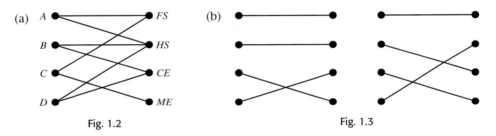

Fig. 1.2   Fig. 1.3

Figure 1.2 shows the graph, and Fig. 1.3 shows the two options.

The maximal matching of Example 1.1.1 covered all of the nodes and each diagram in Fig. 1.3 is called a **complete matching**. A complete matching is not always possible.

Example 1.1.2

Four couples are booked into a small hotel. The Smiths have requested a double room and the Joneses have asked for a double room on the ground floor. The Browns require a twin-bedded room and the Greens will be happy with any room on the ground floor. The hotel manager has just four rooms to assign, three double and one twin-bedded. The twin-bedded room and one of the doubles is on the ground floor. Can the manager satisfy the requirements of all the couples?

The relevant bipartite graph is shown in Fig. 1.4.

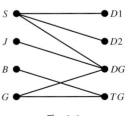

The requirements of the Joneses, Browns and Greens cannot all be satisfied, because the Smiths are the only couple who are content with the double rooms which are not on the ground floor, and they cannot use both of them. The maximal matching has three pairings. One example is $\{S, D1\}$, $\{J, DG\}$, $\{B, TG\}$.

Fig. 1.4

As well as using bipartite graphs to represent the information in assignment problems, you can also use **adjacency matrices**.

The left-nodes are put down one side, and the right-nodes along the top. An entry of 1 means that the corresponding nodes are linked by an arc.

$$\begin{array}{c} \\ S \\ J \\ B \\ G \end{array} \begin{array}{cccc} D1 & D2 & DG & TG \\ \left(\begin{array}{cccc} 1 & 1 & 1 & 0 \\ 0 & 0 & 1 & 0 \\ 0 & 0 & 0 & 1 \\ 0 & 0 & 1 & 1 \end{array}\right) \end{array}$$

Fig. 1.5

For example, the matrix in Fig. 1.5 contains the same information as the graph of Fig. 1.4.

For a problem formulated as an adjacency matrix, the task is to find the maximum number of 1s such that no two of these 1s are in the same row or in the same column. In Fig. 1.6 the solution is shown by the 1s in bold-faced type. If you were solving this problem you would probably wish to circle the 1s in the solution.

$$\left(\begin{array}{cccc} \mathbf{1} & 1 & 1 & 0 \\ 0 & 0 & \mathbf{1} & 0 \\ 0 & 0 & 0 & \mathbf{1} \\ 0 & 0 & 1 & 1 \end{array}\right)$$

Fig. 1.6

1.2 The Matching Augmentation algorithm

In the previous section you solved simple matching problems by inspection. As the numbers of nodes and arcs increase, inspection becomes a hit or miss affair and the chance of overlooking a maximal matching increases.

Fortunately, there is a simple algorithm which can be used to improve upon (or augment) an initial matching or to show that you have already obtained a maximal matching.

Matching Augmentation algorithm

Step 1 Consider all arcs of the matching to be directed from right to left. Consider all other arcs to be directed from left to right.

Step 2 Identify all nodes which do not belong to the matching. Create a new node, X say, joined with directed arcs to all left-nodes which do not belong to the matching.

Step 3 Give each arc a weighting of 1.

Step 4 Apply Dijkstra's algorithm from X until one of the following happens:

• a right-node which does not belong to the matching is reached

• no further labelling is possible. In this case, the initial matching cannot be improved and the algorithm stops.

Step 5 Retrace any path from an unmatched left-node to the unmatched right-node. This is called an alternating path.

Step 6 Remove from the original matching any arcs in the path of Step 5. Add to the matching the other steps in the path. This increases, by 1, the number of arcs in the matching.

Although the following example has only 10 nodes, it is nevertheless difficult to spot a maximal matching. This example will be used to illustrate the Matching Augmentation algorithm.

Example 1.2.1

A builder employs five workers: Alan, who does labouring, plastering and joinery; Betty, who does labouring and wiring; Colin, who does bricklaying and wiring; Di, who does plastering and bricklaying; and Ed, who does plastering, joinery and bricklaying. Can each of the five workers be assigned to a task so that all five tasks are covered?

First, draw a bipartite graph for this problem. In Fig. 1.7, the heavy lines represent a first try at a matching, which assigns just four workers to tasks.

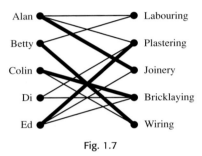

Fig. 1.7

The Matching Augmentation algorithm will show how to improve this matching, if it is possible.

The result of applying the first four steps of the Matching Augmentation algorithm to Example 1.2.1 is shown in Fig. 1.8.

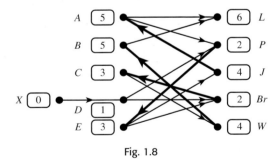

Fig. 1.8

You can see that all the paths have been given directions, as required in Step 1.

The new node X has been created and joined to D, the left-node which does not belong to the initial matching.

Dijkstra's algorithm is then applied from X, and the right-node L, which doesn't belong to the initial matching, is reached. At this stage Step 4 has been completed.

To carry out Step 5, you need to trace a path from D to L: there are two possibilities, D-P-E-J-A-L and D-Br-C-W-B-L, and you could choose either one.

Looking at the first of these, as you trace the path you cover *P-E* and *J-A*, both of which were in the initial matching. Remove them from the initial matching, and add the other arcs from the path, *D-P*, *E-J* and *A-L*, to the initial matching. This increases by 1 the number of arcs in the matching. In this case, the matching is now maximal. It is

$$A\text{-}L, \quad B\text{-}W, \quad C\text{-}Br, \quad D\text{-}P, \quad E\text{-}J.$$

If you had chosen the other path, *D-Br-C-W-B-L*, you would have covered *Br-C* and *W-B* from the initial matching. If you removed them, and added *D-Br*, *C-W* and *B-L* to the original matching, the new matching would be

$$A\text{-}J, \quad B\text{-}L, \quad C\text{-}W, \quad D\text{-}Br, \quad E\text{-}P,$$

an alternative maximal matching.

The next example illustrates how the Matching Augmentation algorithm recognises that a maximal matching has already been reached.

Example 1.2.2

A school timetabling team is trying to timetable four teachers, Andy, Barbara, Chris and Dave to four classes, denoted by *R, S, T* and *U*.

Andy can teach *R* or *S*   Barbara can teach *R, S, T* or *U*
Chris can teach *R* or *S*   Dave can teach *S*.

Draw a bipartite graph and apply the Matching Augmentation algorithm to find a maximal matching.

An initial attempt at a matching is illustrated by the heavy lines in Fig. 1.9.

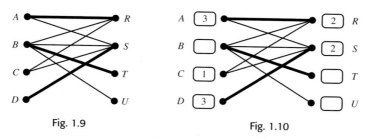

Fig. 1.9   Fig. 1.10

The result of applying the Matching Augmentation algorithm is then shown in Fig. 1.10. The label *X*, that was initially created and then joined to *C* is not shown.

No further labelling is possible, so the initial matching is maximal. Notice that although it is maximal it is not complete.

For an existing non-maximal matching, *M*, of a bipartite graph, *G*, the Matching Augmentation algorithm produces what is called an alternating path.

> An **alternating path** for *M* in *G* is a path which consists alternately of arcs in *M* and arcs not in *M*.

This definition makes it easier to see why the Matching Augmentation algorithm works. The following argument is not a proof, however.

Consider the two situations in which Step 4 of the algorithm stops. If Step 4 stops because no further labelling is possible, the algorithm has shown the initial matching to be maximal. If Step 4 stops because a right-node which isn't in the matching has been reached, Step 6 will improve the matching. In the second case the algorithm has constructed a path from an unmatched left-node to an unmatched right-node. The path is alternating because the only way to go from left to right is via an arc which is not in M, and the only way to go from right to left is via an arc which is in M. Because the path starts at the left and ends at the right it must contain one more arc not in M than in M, and so Step 6 of the algorithm produces a matching that contains one more arc than the initial matching.

Exercise 1A

1 Apply the Matching Augmentation algorithm to the following bipartite graphs where the heavy lines represent matchings. In each case state what you can conclude.

(a) 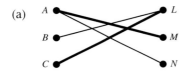   (b)

2 Find the adjacency matrix corresponding to the bipartite graph in the figure.

Select four 1s in the matrix in such a way that no two 1s are in the same row or column. Hence find a maximal matching for the bipartite graph.

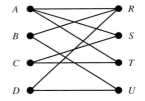

3 A large department store employs five students, Anita, Bruce, Chloe, Darminder and Errol, for the Christmas period.

The Hardware manager would be happy to use Anita, Chloe or Darminder.
The Bookshop manager would be happy to use Bruce or Errol.
The Sports manager would be happy to use Anita or Darminder.
The Electrical manager would be happy to use Darminder or Errol.
The Food hall manager would be happy to use Anita or Chloe.

(a) Draw a bipartite graph, G, to show which students are suitable for each department.

The managing director initially decides to place Anita in the Food hall, Chloe in Hardware, Darminder in Electrical and Errol in the Bookshop. However, he is then unable to place Bruce appropriately.

(b) Show the incomplete matching, M, that describes the managing director's attempted allocation.

(c) Use the Matching Augmentation algorithm to construct an alternating path for M in G, and hence find a complete matching.

4 A dance team consists of four men, Ahmed, Benny, Chris and Derek, paired with four women, Ann, Bala, Celine and Di. Ann is only prepared to dance with Ahmed, Bala will dance with Benny or Derek, Celine will dance with Chris, and Di will dance with any of the men. In their first competition, Di dances with Derek.

(a) Draw a bipartite graph, with the women on the left and the men on the right, to represent the only possible matching with Di and Derek paired.

Unfortunately, Di and Derek fall out and a different pairing has to be arranged for the second competition.

(b) Draw a bipartite graph to show the possible pairings and the incomplete matching, M, from the first competition.

(c) Apply the Matching Augmentation algorithm to obtain a complete matching for the second competition.

1.3* Maximal matching–minimum cover

This section contains extension material and may be omitted.

There is an important connection between the matching problem and the problem of finding sets of nodes which cover every arc, that is sets of nodes which contain at least one end-node of each arc of the bipartite graph. These are called **cover sets** of the graph.

Consider, for example, the graph drawn for Example 1.2.2, redrawn as Fig. 1.11.

Since A-R, B-T and D-S is a matching, a cover set must contain at least one of A or R, at least one of B or T and at least one of D or S.

Fig. 1.11

In general it is clear that:

The number of arcs in any matching	$\leqslant$	the number of nodes in any cover set.

The smallest possible number of nodes in a cover set cannot, therefore, be less than the number of arcs in a maximal matching. In Example 1.2.2, this minimum is actually achieved for the cover set $\{B, R, S\}$. The interesting aspect of the connection between the matching problem and the cover set problem is that this result is always true. That is:

The number of arcs in a maximal matching	$=$	the minimum number of nodes in a cover set.

This is called the maximal matching–minimum cover result.

You can prove this result by considering the effect of applying the Matching Augmentation algorithm to bipartite graphs for which the maximal matching has already been achieved.

First, consider the following examples:

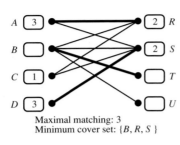

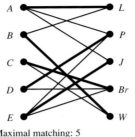

Maximal matching: 3
Minimum cover set: {B, R, S }

Fig. 1.12

Maximal matching: 5
Minimum cover set: {A, B, C, D, E }

Fig. 1.13

The key to proving the maximal matching–minimum cover result is to note how the examples of cover sets in Figs. 1.12 to 1.14 are formed. In each case, they consist of the unlabelled left-nodes and labelled right-nodes.

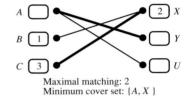

Maximal matching: 2
Minimum cover set: {A, X }

Fig. 1.14

To prove the maximal matching–minimum cover result it is therefore necessary to prove:

- the unlabelled left-nodes and labelled right-nodes form a cover set;
- the number of these nodes equals the number of arcs in a maximal matching.

These two facts follow from the following features of maximal matchings to which the Matching Augmentation algorithm has been applied. In each case, you should try to explain the reason for these features (see Miscellaneous exercise 1 Question 12).

- Each arc of the bipartite graph either has an unlabelled left-node or a labelled right-node.
- All unlabelled left-nodes are in the matching.
- All labelled right-nodes are in the matching.
- Each arc of the matching joins nodes which are either both labelled or both unlabelled.

Then:

Number of arcs of maximal matching

= number of right-nodes of matching

= number of unlabelled right-nodes of matching
+ number of labelled right-nodes of matching

= number of unlabelled left-nodes of matching
+ number of labelled right-nodes of matching

= number of unlabelled left-nodes + number of labelled right-nodes.

Each arc of the bipartite graph has either an unlabelled left-node or a labelled right-node, but not both. So the set of unlabelled left-nodes and labelled right-nodes is a cover set. It must be a minimum cover set since it has the same number of nodes as the number of arcs in a matching.

The maximal matching–minimum cover result can be useful for seeing quickly that you have found a maximal matching and need not apply the Matching Augmentation algorithm.

Example 1.3.1

For the bipartite graph shown in Fig. 1.15, find

(a) a cover set containing four nodes,

(b) a matching containing four arcs.

What can you conclude about your answers to (a) and (b)?

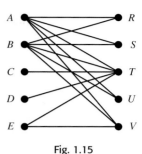

Fig. 1.15

    (a) A, B, T, V.

    (b) $\{A, R\}$, $\{B, S\}$, $\{C, T\}$, $\{E, V\}$.

A cover set and a matching of the same sizes have been found. The solution to part (a) is therefore a minimum cover set and the solution to part (b) is a maximal matching.

1.4 Allocation problems

Suppose that a building company has four contracts which must be completed at the same time. The work is to be done by subcontractors, each of whom can carry out only one contract. The subcontractors' quotes for each of the four jobs are shown in Table 1.16.

		Contract			
		A	B	C	D
Subcontractor	1	10	5	9	–
	2	9	6	9	6
	3	10	–	10	7
	4	9	5	9	8

Quotes are in £1000s.
'–' indicates no quote.

Table 1.16

Here there is no difficulty in finding a matching. An example is 1-*A*, 2-*B*, 3-*C*, 4-*D*. The problem is to find a matching which minimises the total cost; such a problem is called an **allocation problem**.

A good method of tackling allocation problems is to reduce the array of costs by subtracting from each element of a row (or column) the least element in that row (or column). For example, Table 1.18 is obtained from Table 1.17 by subtracting 5, 6, 7 and 5 from the first, second, third and fourth rows respectively. The smallest number in each new row is now equal to zero.

10	5	9	–	$-5 \rightarrow$
9	6	9	6	$-6 \rightarrow$
10	–	10	7	$-7 \rightarrow$
9	5	9	8	$-5 \rightarrow$

Table 1.17

5	0	4	–
3	0	3	0
3	–	3	0
4	0	4	8

Table 1.18

The solution to the original problem will then simply be the solution to the new problem with an extra cost of £23,000 because $5 + 6 + 7 + 5 = 23$. Reducing the columns of Table 1.18 in a similar way, in this case by subtracting 3 from the first and third columns, leads to the array in Table 1.19.

2	0	1	—
0	0	0	0
0	—	0	0
1	0	1	3

Table 1.19

For this matrix, it is easy to see that there are no matchings of zero cost but there are several of cost only 1. For example, Table 1.20 shows a matching of cost 1 in bold type.

2	**0**	1	—
0	0	**0**	0
0	—	0	**0**
1	0	1	3

Table 1.20

So the original problem has an optimal allocation, of cost £30,000, shown in Table 1.21.

10	**5**	9	—
9	6	**9**	6
10	—	10	**7**
9	5	9	8

Table 1.21

> To solve an allocation problem, first reduce the array of costs by subtracting the least number in a row (or column) from each element of that row (or column).

Example 1.4.1

Choose five numbers from the array given below so that the sum of the five numbers is the least possible. No two numbers can be in the same row or column.

10	10	9	8	10
10	12	12	9	13
16	16	14	12	15
14	15	12	12	16
15	16	14	13	14

Reducing the array by rows leads to the array on the left; then reducing by columns leads to the array on the right, in which the minimum allocation is shown in bold type.

2	2	1	0	2	1	**0**	1	0	1
1	3	3	0	4	**0**	1	3	0	3
4	4	2	0	3	3	2	2	**0**	2
2	3	0	0	4	1	1	**0**	0	3
2	3	1	0	1	1	1	1	0	**0**

For the original array the pattern indicated by the emboldened numbers yields the minimum allocation of

$$10 + 10 + 12 + 12 + 14 = 58.$$

Having negative numbers in the array does not affect the method because the stage of 'subtracting the least number in a row from each element of that row' will make all elements at least zero. For example, in Table 1.22 each element has -3 subtracted from it, which is just the same as adding 3 to each element.

8	-3	4	7	$-(-3)$ or $+ 3 \rightarrow$	11	0	7	10

Table 1.22

To maximise an allocation you can therefore simply change the sign of every element and then minimise in the usual way, as in Table 1.23.

3	1	2	Change sign $\rightarrow$	-3	-1	-2	$-(-3) \rightarrow$	0	2	1

Table 1.23

The same effect is produced by subtracting each element from the largest value in the array, shown in Table 1.24.

3	1	2	Subtract from 3 $\rightarrow$	0	2	1

Table 1.24

The next example illustrates this process.

Example 1.4.2
Choose five numbers from the array given below so that the sum of the five numbers is the greatest possible. No two numbers can be in the same row or column.

10	10	9	8	10
10	12	12	9	13
16	16	14	12	15
14	15	12	12	16
15	16	14	13	14

First, convert the problem to a standard minimising one by changing the sign of each element of the array or by subtracting each element from 16. Reducing by rows then gives:

0	0	1	2	0
3	1	1	4	0
0	0	2	4	1
2	1	4	4	0
1	0	2	3	2

Reducing by columns gives:

0	0	0	**0**	0
3	1	**0**	2	0
0	0	1	2	1
2	1	3	2	**0**
1	**0**	1	1	2

The numbers in bold type show the minimum allocation. For the original array the same pattern yields the maximum allocation of $16 + 16 + 12 + 8 + 16 = 68$.

1.5   The Hungarian algorithm

The opening example of Section 1.4 led to the reduced array in Table 1.25.

2	0	1	—
0	0	0	0
0	—	0	0
1	0	1	3

Table 1.25

At this stage you had to 'spot' that an allocation of four zeros was impossible and that it was necessary to use a 1. In larger and more complicated examples it is better to have a systematic procedure. One such method, called the **Hungarian algorithm**, is based upon the ideas of Section 1.3 and depends upon covering the zero elements with the minimum number of vertical or horizontal lines or both.

In this case, three lines are needed, shown in Table 1.26.

Table 1.26

Note the least uncovered element, in this case 1. Add this element to the elements of each covered row and then to the elements of each covered column. Where an element is covered twice, add the least uncovered element twice. See Table 1.27 for the result of this process.

2	1	1	—
1	2	1	1
1	—	1	1
1	1	1	3

Table 1.27

Then subtract this element from every element of the array. The result is shown in Table 1.28.

1	0	0	—
0	1	0	0
0	—	0	0
0	0	0	2

Table 1.28

1	**0**	0	—
0	1	0	0
0	—	0	**0**
0	0	**0**	2

Table 1.29

It is now possible to allocate four zeros in several ways; one is shown by the numbers in bold type in Table 1.29. This pattern, applied to the original array, yields the minimum value of $9 + 5 + 9 + 7 = 30$, that is £30,000.

The reason that this procedure further reduces the array is that the minimum number is added on $3 \times 4 = 12$ times but is then subtracted 16 times. The following statement of the Hungarian algorithm shortens this procedure.

Hungarian algorithm

Step 1 Reduce the array of costs by both row and column subtractions.

Step 2 Cover the zero elements with the minimum number of lines. If this minimum number is the same as the size of the array (which for a square matrix means the number of rows) then go to Step 4.

Step 3 Let m be the minimum uncovered element. The array is augmented by reducing all uncovered elements by m and increasing all elements covered by two lines by m. Return to Step 2. This process is called **augmenting the elements**.

Step 4 There is a maximal matching using only zeros. Apply this pattern to the original array.

Example 1.5.1

A company has four sales representatives to allocate to four groups of retailers. The table shows the estimated weekly mileage of each representative when assigned a particular group. How should the groups be allocated to minimise the total mileage?

	1	2	3	4
Alex	280	280	260	210
Ben	470	480	460	420
Charles	370	390	380	330
Davinia	220	250	240	220

The array on the right shows the situation after Step 1, after row and column reductions. The numbers are tens of miles.

The array below on the left shows the situation after Step 2, where two lines are needed to cover the zeros. The array below on the right shows Step 3, where 2, the minimum uncovered element, has been subtracted from all uncovered elements, and elements covered by two lines have been increased by 2. After this, the algorithm returns to Step 2.

$$
\begin{array}{cccc}
7 & 4 & 3 & 0 \\
5 & 3 & 2 & 0 \\
4 & 3 & 3 & 0 \\
0 & 0 & 0 & 0
\end{array}
$$

$$
\begin{array}{cccc}
7 & 4 & 3 & 0 \\
5 & 3 & 2 & 0 \\
4 & 3 & 3 & 0 \\
0 & 0 & 0 & 0
\end{array}
\qquad
\begin{array}{cccc}
5 & 2 & 1 & 0 \\
3 & 1 & 0 & 0 \\
2 & 1 & 1 & 0 \\
0 & 0 & 0 & 2
\end{array}
$$

Steps 2 and 3 are carried out again, as before.

$$
\begin{array}{cccc}
5 & 2 & 1 & 0 \\
3 & 1 & 0 & 0 \\
2 & 1 & 1 & 0 \\
0 & 0 & 0 & 2
\end{array}
\qquad
\begin{array}{cccc}
4 & 1 & 0 & 0 \\
3 & 1 & 0 & 1 \\
1 & 0 & 0 & 0 \\
0 & 0 & 0 & 3
\end{array}
$$

At this stage, carrying out Step 2 requires four lines. As this is the same as the size of the array, you can go to Step 4, where the pattern of zeros is shown in bold type.

$$
\begin{array}{cccc}
4 & 1 & 0 & 0 \\
3 & 1 & 0 & 1 \\
1 & 0 & 0 & 0 \\
0 & 0 & 0 & 3
\end{array}
\qquad
\begin{array}{cccc}
4 & 1 & 0 & \mathbf{0} \\
3 & 1 & \mathbf{0} & 1 \\
1 & \mathbf{0} & 0 & 0 \\
\mathbf{0} & 0 & 0 & 3
\end{array}
$$

Using the pattern of zeros, the optimum allocation is 1-Davinia, 2-Charles, 3-Ben, 4-Alex, with mileage $220 + 390 + 460 + 210 = 1280$.

The dependence of the Hungarian algorithm upon the minimum number of lines covering zeros is explained in the starred Section 1.3. If the maximal matching is shown in the form of an adjacency matrix, zero-cost arcs are represented by entries of zero. A maximal matching is required, so the minimum cover is needed.

1.6 Non-square arrays

Suppose that five workers are available for four tasks. The times each worker would take at each task are given in Table 1.30. How can each task be allocated to a different worker to minimise the total time?

	1	2	3	4
Angel	170	220	190	200
Britney	140	230	150	160
Cleo	180	210	170	170
Dimitri	190	240	210	220
Ed	160	220	170	170

Table 1.30

To be able to apply the methods of this chapter it is first necessary to create a square array by adding in a dummy column.

The trick is to add in a column of equal numbers so that this column does not influence the choice of workers for the other tasks. It is conventional (but not necessary) to make these numbers equal to the largest number in the array. This technique is shown in the next example.

Example 1.6.1

Select four numbers from the array given below so that the sum of the four numbers is the least possible. No two numbers can be in the same row or column.

170	220	190	200
140	230	150	160
180	210	170	170
190	240	210	220
160	220	170	170

Add in a column of 240s to obtain a square array.

170	220	190	200	240
140	230	150	160	240
180	210	170	170	240
190	240	210	220	240
160	220	170	170	240

Reducing rows and then columns, and dividing by 10, so that the entries are in tens, gives the following array, which requires three lines to cover the zeros.

0	1	2	3	2
0	5	1	2	5
1	0	0	0	2
0	1	2	3	0
0	2	1	1	3

After covering the first column, and the third and fourth rows, and augmenting the elements (only one return to Step 2 is required), you obtain the following array in which the zeros in each row and column are in bold type.

0	**0**	1	2	1
0	4	**0**	1	4
2	0	0	**0**	2
1	1	2	3	**0**
0	1	0	0	2

The solution to the original problem is $160 + 220 + 150 + 170 = 700$.

> To apply the Hungarian algorithm to a non-square array, first add in dummy rows or columns to make the numbers of rows and columns equal.

Exercise 1B

1 The four members of a swimming relay team must, between them, swim 100 metres of each of backstroke, breaststroke, butterfly and crawl.

Five hopefuls for the team have personal best times as follows.

	Back	Breast	Butterfly	Crawl	
A	66	68	71	60	
B	69	69	72	60	
C	68	70	73	61	Times in seconds
D	65	66	71	63	for 100 metres.
E	63	65	74	60	

(a) Convert the array into a square one to which the Hungarian algorithm can be applied.

(b) Hence find which four swimmers should be chosen and the stroke for which each should be used.

2 The scores of the four members of a quiz team on practice questions are as follows.

	Sport	Music	Literature	Science
Ali	16	18	17	14
Bea	19	17	14	18
Chris	12	16	16	15
Deepan	11	15	17	14

A different person needs to be picked for each of the four different topics.

(a) How could the table be altered in order to use the Hungarian algorithm?

(b) Hence allocate the topics to the members of the team.

3 Apply the Hungarian algorithm to find the minimum possible total of six numbers, chosen from the table below in such a way that no two numbers lie in the same row or column.

3	2	1	3	1	2
2	1	3	1	2	3
3	4	5	2	5	3
4	3	2	1	3	4
5	4	3	3	2	3
3	1	4	1	2	1

4 Find the maximum possible total for six numbers chosen as in Question 3.

5 Suppose that the Hungarian algorithm is being applied to an array.

(a) Suppose further that the zeros in a 5×5 array are covered by three lines and the least non-covered element is a 2. When the array is augmented once, what is the reduction in the total of all the elements?

(b) Suppose that the zeros of an $n \times n$ array are covered by k lines and that the least non-covered element is l. What is the reduction in the total of all elements when this array is augmented once?

6 A builder has four labourers who must be assigned to four tasks. The estimates of the times each labourer would take for the different tasks are as shown in the table.

	Task			
	1	2	3	4
A	3	4	4	3
B	3	3	1	2
C	4	3	2	4
D	4	1	2	3

Times in hours.

Given that no labourer can be assigned to more than one task, use the Hungarian algorithm to find the optimum assignment.

Miscellaneous exercise 1

1 In a mixed badminton tournament, four men, Arnold, Barry, Charles and Derek, must be paired with four women, Jane, Kate, Lorna and Marie.

- Arnold may be paired with Jane, Kate or Lorna, but not Marie.
- Barry may be paired with Kate only.
- Charles may be paired with Kate or Marie, but not Jane or Lorna.
- Derek may be paired with Jane or Marie, but not Kate or Lorna.

(a) Draw a bipartite graph, G, showing which men may be paired with which women.

Jane decides to pair with Arnold, Kate decides to pair with Barry and Marie decides to pair with Derek. This leaves Lorna and Charles, who will not agree to be paired.

(b) On your graph, G, show the incomplete matching, M, described above.

(c) Use a matching algorithm to construct an alternating path for M in G, explaining your method carefully, and hence obtain a complete matching between the men and the women.   (OCR)

2 Jim is spending a week on holiday at Spaceworld. The table lists the planets that he wants to visit, and the days that these planets are open for visitors. Jim wants to visit one planet each day.

Mercury	Saturday and Monday
Venus	Saturday, Sunday and Monday
Earth	Monday, Tuesday and Wednesday
Mars	Monday and Friday
Jupiter	Wednesday and Thursday
Saturn	Tuesday
Uranus	Sunday and Friday

Jim arrived at Spaceworld on Saturday, and immediately went to visit Mercury. On Sunday he visited Venus and on Monday he visited Earth.

Jim then realised that he would not be able to visit all seven planets on his list in the week. He decided that he would leave out visiting Uranus, and that he would have a free day on Thursday.

(a) Draw a bipartite graph showing which planets are open on which days, and use it to show the incomplete matching that Jim chose.

(b) Use a matching algorithm to construct an alternating path, and hence find a maximal matching between the planets and the days.   (OCR)

3 Granny has bought Christmas presents for her five grandchildren.

> The teddy bear is suitable for Cathy, Daniel or Elvis;
> the book is suitable for Annie or Ben;
> the football is suitable for Daniel or Elvis;
> the money box is suitable for Annie or Daniel;
> the drum is suitable for Cathy or Elvis.

Draw a bipartite graph, G, to show which present is suitable for which grandchild.

Granny decides to give Annie the book, Cathy the teddy bear, Daniel the money box and Elvis the drum. This leaves Ben without a present, since the football is not suitable for him.

(a) Show the incomplete matching, M, that describes which present Granny has decided to give to each child.

(b) Use a matching algorithm to construct an alternating path for M in G, and hence find a maximal matching between the presents and the grandchildren.   (OCR, adapted)

4 Four children are choosing sandwiches.

The four sandwiches available are one bacon, one cheese, one egg and one fishpaste sandwich.

Each child must get one of the four sandwiches, and each sandwich must be given to one child.

Jemma would like bacon or cheese, Kay would like cheese or egg, Luke would like cheese or fishpaste, and Matthew would like bacon or fishpaste.

(a) Draw a bipartite graph, G, showing which children would like which sandwiches.

Jemma chooses bacon, Kay chooses cheese and Luke chooses fishpaste.

(b) Show this incomplete matching, M, on your graph G.

(c) Use a matching algorithm to construct an alternating path for M in G, explaining your method carefully, and hence obtain a complete matching between the children and the sandwiches.   (OCR)

5 Four workers are to be allocated to four jobs. The cost, in £1000s, of using each worker for each job is shown in the table.

		Job			
		Building	Carpentry	Drainage	Electrics
	Jenny	4	3	2	7
	Kenny	3	2	3	4
Worker	Lenny	6	3	4	5
	Penny	7	7	7	6

(a) Use the Hungarian algorithm to pair the four workers with the four jobs to minimise the total cost.

(b) Give the minimum total cost.   (OCR)

6 Four house building companies, 1, 2, 3 and 4, are invited to tender for the construction of four different types of house *L, M, S, T*. Each company estimates the price it would charge. This information is shown in the table in £1000s.

		House type			
		L	*M*	*S*	*T*
Company	1	40	35	24	21
	2	38	44	28	16
	3	44	42	26	22
	4	43	39	40	20

Regulations prevent a building company from constructing more than one type of house.

(a) Use the Hungarian algorithm, by applying column reductions first, to determine which company should build which house if the total cost is to be a minimum.

(b) Calculate the minimum cost.   (OCR)

7 Donna Wyg runs a detective agency. She has been employed to follow a suspect and needs to choose a different disguise for each day. Donna estimates that the job will last four days. She can choose from five disguises.

Past experience has shown that some disguises are more appropriate than others for certain locations. She knows the likely locations of the suspect on each day.

The table shows the probability that Donna will be spotted in each of the disguises at each of the locations.

Day	Location	Disguise				
		Artist	Bag lady	Cleaner	Duchess	Expert
Wednesday	Waxworks	0.12	0.24	0.12	0.44	0.18
Thursday	Theatre	0.14	0.27	0.10	0.46	0.43
Friday	Fair	0.16	0.23	0.13	0.45	0.51
Saturday	Station	0.14	0.22	0.11	0.47	0.12

Donna wants to choose the disguises so that the sum of the probabilities of being spotted is as small as possible. To do this she will use the Hungarian algorithm.

(a) The Hungarian algorithm requires the number of rows and columns to be equal. Add an appropriate dummy row to the probability matrix to make it square.

(b) By reducing columns first, find a reduced probability matrix and explain how you know whether it gives a minimum probability allocation.

(c) Write down a list showing which disguise Donna should choose for each day.   (OCR)

8 The headmaster of a primary school is well-known for the strange combinations of shirt colours and tie patterns that he chooses. One day he brings four shirts and four ties to school and asks the children, by voting, to help him pair the ties with the shirts.

The number of votes cast against each combination is shown in the table.

		Tie pattern			
		Circles	Diamonds	Flowers	Gaudy
Shirt	Purple	5	7	12	26
	Orange	8	3	18	21
	Red	3	10	15	22
	Yellow	5	6	14	25

Use an appropriate algorithm to pair the four shirts with the four tie patterns so as to minimise the total number of votes against.   (OCR)

9 Simon is planning a four-day break. He wants to spend one day at the art gallery, one day at the beach, one day at the castle and one day at the exhibition.

The cost, in £, for Simon to visit each of these places on each of the four days is shown in the table.

	Art gallery	Beach	Castle	Exhibition
Wednesday	5.00	1.50	4.50	6.30
Thursday	4.50	1.20	5.00	6.00
Friday	5.00	1.50	5.00	6.00
Saturday	6.00	1.50	5.50	7.00

(a) Use the Hungarian algorithm to pair the four places with the four days so as to minimise Simon's total cost.

(b) Give the minimum total cost.   (OCR)

10* A bipartite graph has the following adjacency matrix, where each non-zero entry corresponds to an arc.

$$\begin{array}{c} \\ A \\ B \\ C \\ D \end{array} \begin{array}{cccc} R & S & T & U \\ \left(\begin{array}{cccc} 0 & 0 & 1 & 0 \\ 1 & 0 & 1 & 1 \\ 0 & 1 & 0 & 0 \\ 0 & 1 & 1 & 0 \end{array} \right) \end{array}$$

(a) Find three horizontal or vertical lines which cover every non-zero entry.

(b) Find a matching of three pairs of nodes.

(c) What is the size of a maximal matching? Explain your answer.

11 Granny is on holiday and wants to send postcards to her five grandchildren. She has chosen six postcards and has given each card a score to show how suitable it is for each grandchild. A high score means that the card is more suitable.

		Card					
		Maps	Puppies	Railway	Seaside	Teddies	Views
	Arnie	5	0	4	1	0	3
	Beth	3	1	0	1	0	3
Grandchild	Cyril	0	3	2	3	2	1
	Des	3	2	2	3	2	2
	Erin	1	2	3	3	1	2

(a) The Hungarian algorithm finds the allocation with minimum total cost. Show how Granny's problem can be converted into a minimisation problem.

(b) The Hungarian algorithm requires the matrix to be square. Explain how to represent Granny's problem as a square matrix.

(c) Use the Hungarian algorithm, reducing columns first, to pair the cards to the grandchildren in the most appropriate way. (OCR)

12* The Matching Augmentation algorithm is applied to a bipartite graph for which the maximal matching has already been obtained. Explain why

(a) each arc of the bipartite graph either has an unlabelled left-node or a labelled right-node,

(b) all unlabelled left-nodes are in the matching,

(c) all labelled right-nodes are in the matching,

(d) each arc of the matching joins nodes which are either both labelled or both unlabelled.

2 Network flows

This chapter is about maximising the flow through a network. When you have completed it you should

- know how to represent flow problems by networks with directed arcs
- understand and know how to apply the maximum flow–minimum cut theorem
- know how to find a maximum flow in a network, subject to given constraints (including both upper and lower capacities), by using a labelling procedure to augment a given flow
- be able to deal with multiple sources and sinks, and with nodes with restricted capacities.

2.1 Some important terms

Problems involving flows through networks are widespread. They include the movement of traffic through an airport, the flow of oil in a system of pipes and the transfer of information across the internet.

Consider the problem of finding the maximum number of cars that can enter and leave the road network shown in Fig. 2.1.

The weights on the arcs are called **capacities**. The start of the network is called the **source**, and is often labelled *S*. The end of the network is called the **sink**, and is often labelled *T*.

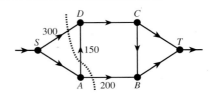

Fig. 2.1

For the problem above, you may have spotted a flow such as that in Fig. 2.2 which gives a total throughput of 650 cars per hour. In this solution, arcs which are carrying their full capacity, such as *SD* and *CB*, are said to be **saturated**.

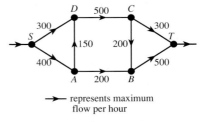

Fig. 2.2

There is a simple way of seeing that this flow is the maximum possible by making a suitable **cut** across the entire network.

A **cut** is any continuous line which separates *S* from *T*. A cut must not pass through any nodes.

In Fig. 2.3 the maximum possible flow across the cut line in the direction from *S* to *T* (called the **value**, or **capacity**, of the cut) is $300 + 150 + 200 = 650$ so this flow cannot be bettered unless the capacities of at least one of the roads *SD*, *AD* or *AB* is increased.

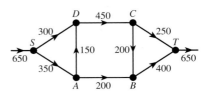

Fig. 2.3

You should note that, throughout this chapter, it will be assumed that there can be no 'build-up' at a node. That is, with the exception of the source and sink, the sum of the flows into a node must be equal to the sum of the flows out of that node.

2.2   Maximum flow–minimum cut theorem

Any cut across a network can be thought of as a collection of potential bottlenecks which restrict the flow through the network.

Figure 2.4 is an example of a cut, with five arcs crossing it. Four of them, a, b, d and e, have flows from the source to the sink, but one of them, c, is in the reverse direction.

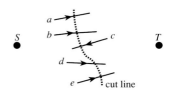

Fig. 2.4

The value of any cut limits the maximum possible flow. In this case the maximum flow cannot exceed $a + b + d + e$. Note that c is not included in the value of the cut because it is a flow in the wrong direction.

You have therefore seen that

the value of any permissible flow $\leqslant$ the value of any particular cut.

In particular

the maximum flow $\leqslant$ the value of the minimum cut.

This result should remind you of the results of Section 1.3, where equality actually held. The same is true here. It can be proved that the maximum flow equals the value of the minimum cut.

> **Maximum flow–minimum cut theorem**
>
> (a) The flow through a network cannot exceed the value of any cut.
>
> (b) The maximum flow equals the value of the minimum cut.

This theorem does not actually provide you with an algorithm to find the maximum flow. It does, however, give you a useful tactic when considering relatively simple networks.

> If you can find, by inspection, a flow and a cut which have the same value, then the maximum flow–minimum cut theorem tells you that you have obtained the maximum flow.

Example 2.2.1

(a) Find the value of the cut shown in the diagram.

(b) Find a flow with the same capacity as the value found in part (a). What can you deduce?

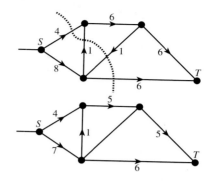

  (a) The value of the cut is $4 + 1 + 6 = 11$.

  (b) This is the maximum possible flow.

Exercise 2A

1 Find the values of the four cuts shown in the diagram. What can you deduce about the maximum flow?

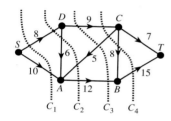

2 (a) Find the maximum flow through this network.

 (b) Prove your answer cannot be exceeded by finding a cut of the same value.

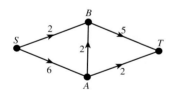

3 The numbers on the arcs in the diagram represent the maximum numbers of passengers, in 1000s per day, who can be carried between five airports.

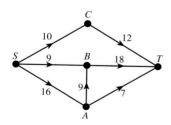

(a) What is the maximum number of passengers per day who can get to T from S?

(b) If the capacity of only one connection can be increased, which one should it be?

4 (a) Find the cut of minimum value for the network shown in the diagram.

   (b) How do you know your answer to part (a) is the minimum?

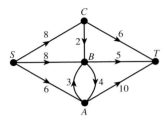

5 For the network shown, find a number k such that there is both a flow of k from S to T and a cut of value k.

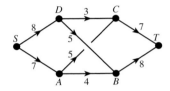

2.3   The labelling procedure

So far you have no algorithm to find the maximum flow in a large and complicated network. This section introduces an algorithm which can be used to systematically augment, that is improve, any initial flow. Note that there is no problem about finding an initial flow, because you can start with flows of zero!

To illustrate the procedure, first consider a very simple example. Figure 2.5 shows a network with the maximum capacity shown for each arc.

Start with an initial flow of 5 along S-A-B-T. The next step is to redraw the network, indicating the amounts by which the flow along each arc could be altered.

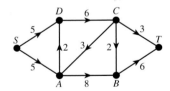

Fig. 2.5

For example, AB has a flow of 5 and a capacity of 8, so the flow from A to B could be increased by 3 from 5 to 8, or decreased by 5 from 5 to 0. AB is therefore redrawn as shown in Fig. 2.6. Similarly, AD has a flow of 0 and a capacity of 2, so it is redrawn as shown in Fig. 2.7.

You should then obtain the new network shown in Fig. 2.8, which is the **network of possible increases** (excess capacities, or 'how much more', and potential backflows, or 'how much less') associated with the original network and initial flow.

Fig. 2.6   Fig. 2.7

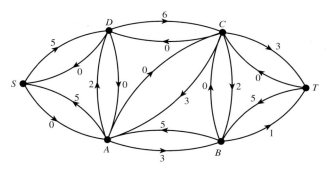

Fig. 2.8

You then find *any* flow from S to T on this new network. For example, you can see that a flow of 3 on *S-D-C-T* is possible. Adjust the labellings as shown in Fig. 2.9.

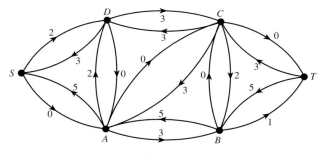

Fig. 2.9

You can now find another flow, 1 on *S-D-C-B-T*. Adjust the labellings again, as in Fig. 2.10.

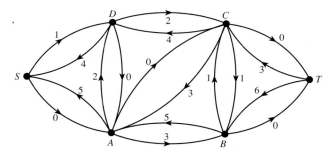

Fig. 2.10

If you look at the arcs into T which show how much the capacity can be increased, you will see that they are both labelled 0. The original arcs into T have become saturated. In the network of increases, S and T are now disconnected, so there can be no extra flow from S to T.

Therefore the maximum flow is the sum of 5 on *S-A-B-T*, 3 on *S-D-C-T* and 1 on *S-D-C-B-T*.

Here is the full algorithm.

> ### Labelling procedure
>
> **Step 1** Begin with any initial flow or zero flow.
>
> **Step 2** Replace each arc with two arcs, one showing the amount by which the flow can be increased (its excess capacity) and the other showing the amount by which the flow can be decreased (its potential backflow).
>
> **Step 3** If S is still connected to T (this can be determined by Dijkstra's algorithm if it is not obvious) then find a new flow from S to T and alter the excess capacities and potential backflows as necessary.
>
> **Step 4** Repeat Step 3 until S is disconnected from T.
>
> If S is disconnected from T then the maximum flow is the sum of all the flows of Steps 1 and 3.

Note that, at the end of the labelling procedure, the maximum flow can also be found by subtracting the excess capacities leaving the source from the original capacities leaving the source, or by doing the same with the sink.

Thus the original capacity leaving the source was 10, and the excess capacity is now 1. This leaves the maximum flow as 9. You can check for yourself that the same is true for the sink.

Example 2.3.1
The first diagram shows the maximum capacities of arcs in a network and the second diagram shows the flows currently established.

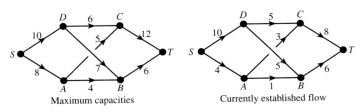

Maximum capacities   Currently established flow

(a) Find a minimum cut and give its value.

(b) Explain how you know that the established flows are not maximum.

(c) Apply the labelling procedure to augment the flows and find a set of maximum flows.

(a) The cut {DC, AC, BT} has a value of 17.

(b) The maximum flow must be 17 whereas the established flow is only 14.

(c)

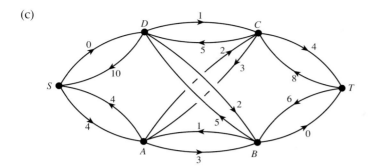

Augment the flow by 2 on S-A-C-T and by another 1 on S-A-B-D-C-T.

The flow now has value 17 and therefore must be maximum. The final maximum flows are shown in the figure on the right.

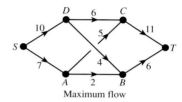

Maximum flow

2.4   Extensions

In practical applications, the methods developed in this chapter often need to be extended to cope with variations such as multiple sources or multiple sinks or both; nodes of restricted capacity; and arcs with lower as well as upper capacities. For example, an oil pipeline system may have multiple inflows and multiple outflows; high-capacity roads may pass through a village where road works restrict capacity; a conduit may need a minimum level of use in order to remain free-flowing. This section and the next one will illustrate how you can tackle such problems.

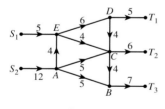

Fig. 2.11

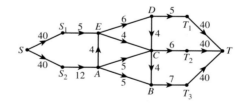

Fig. 2.12

Consider the network shown in Fig. 2.11. It has two sources, S_1 and S_2, and three sinks, T_1, T_2 and T_3.

In order to apply the methods of this chapter create a new **supersource**, S, that feeds the existing sources with capacities sufficiently big so as not to affect the solution. Similarly, create a new **supersink**, T. The new network obtained is shown in Fig. 2.12.

You can now apply the standard methods to the new network. The cut through S_1E and S_2A has value 17. Any flow of this value will therefore be a maximum flow. You can then obtain a maximum flow on the original network from this flow by removing the supersource and supersink, as shown in Fig. 2.13.

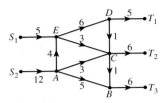

Fig. 2.13

If a network has more than one source, then create a new supersource.

If a network has more than one sink, then create a new supersink.

To this point, flows in a network have only been constrained by the capacities of the arcs in the network. However, it is also common for flows to be restricted by the capacities of nodes. Suppose a network models foot traffic through a building where the arcs represent corridors and the nodes represent doorways. A realistic analysis of flows through this network may have to consider that some of the doors are security or fire doors and, as a result, restrict the number of people who can pass through the building in a given amount of time.

Example 2.4.1
In the network shown in the diagram, node B has a restricted capacity of 8. Find the maximum possible flow.

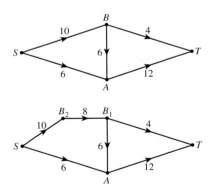

Replace node B by a pair of nodes B_1 and B_2, linked by an arc of capacity 8.

The minimum cut for the new network is 14, so this is also the maximum flow value.

If a node has a restricted capacity then replace it by two unrestricted nodes connected by an arc of the relevant capacity.

2.5 Minimum capacities

Sometimes, a minimum flow is essential along one or more of the arcs. In such cases it is conventional to label each directed arc with two numbers, an upper capacity and a lower capacity. An example is shown in Fig. 2.14.

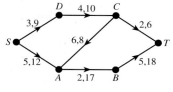

For such a network, the value of a cut is defined as follows.

Fig. 2.14

> The value of a cut is the sum of the upper capacities for arcs that cross the cut line in the direction from S to T minus the sum of the lower capacities for arcs that cross the cut line in the direction from T to S.

With this definition of the value of a cut, the maximum flow–minimum cut theorem can be applied to networks with both minimum and maximum capacities.

Example 2.5.1

(a) Find the values of the three cuts shown in the network.

(b) Find the maximum flow and the minimum cut.

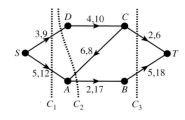

(a) Using the definition in the shaded box, the values of the cuts C_1 and C_3 are $12 + 9 = 21$ and $18 + 6 = 24$ respectively.

The cut C_2 has an arc AC flowing from T to S with a minimum capacity of 6 which must be subtracted. This means that the value of C_2 is $9 - 6 + 17 = 20$.

(b) A flow of 20 is given by

S-D-C	with capacity	9
S-A	with capacity	11
C-A	with capacity	6
A-B-T	with capacity	17
C-T	with capacity	3.

Because there is a cut with this value this is the maximum flow, and C_2 is the minimum cut.

The labelling procedure of Section 2.3 can be used without alteration with minimum as well as maximum capacities, except that you must now start with some initial feasible flow rather than zero flow.

Example 2.5.2

Apply the labelling procedure to the network of Example 2.5.1, repeated as Fig. 2.15, to augment the initial flow given in Fig. 2.16.

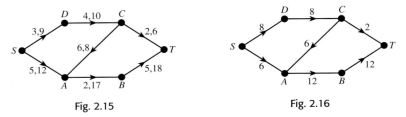

Fig. 2.15   Fig. 2.16

The network of increases associated with this example is shown in Fig. 2.17. This time the backflows are calculated using the minimum capacities. Thus, looking at the arc SD, where there is a minimum capacity of 3, the greatest amount by which the flow of 8 can be reduced is 5.

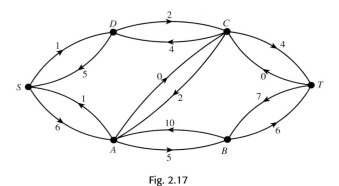

Fig. 2.17

The initial flow can be augmented by a flow of 5 on S-A-B-T and by a flow of 1 on S-D-C-T.

You can check that this labelling procedure gives the solution obtained in Example 2.5.1(b).

Exercise 2B

1 The diagrams below represent capacities and an initial flow. Draw a diagram showing excess capacities and potential backflows.

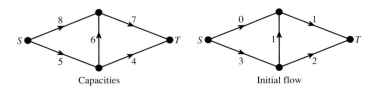

Capacities   Initial flow

2 The diagrams below represent lower and upper capacities, and an initial flow. Draw a diagram showing excess capacities and potential backflows.

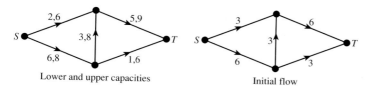

Lower and upper capacities   Initial flow

3 In this network of flows, the arcs have unlimited capacities but the nodes have lower and upper capacities as shown.

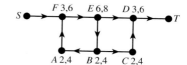

(a) Redraw the network in a form to which you could apply the maximum flow–minimum cut theorem.

(b) Find both a maximum flow and a minimum cut.

4 Redraw the network shown with two extra nodes: a supersource and a supersink.

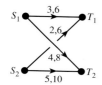

5 In the network shown, S represents an oil field, T a refinery and the other nodes are intermediate stations. Each arc depicts a pipeline through which oil can travel, the capacities being in millions of barrels per hour. Use the labelling procedure to find the maximum number of barrels per hour which can be moved to the refinery.

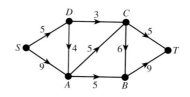

6 The diagram shows a system of pipes with lower and upper capacities.

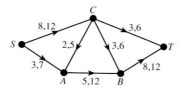

(a) Find a flow of 11 from S to T.

(b) Use the labelling procedure to augment the flow of part (a). Hence find the maximum flow from S to T.

(c) Find a cut of value equal to the maximum flow.

7 EZ-Fly has had to cancel its direct flight from Glasgow to Luton. The number of seats available on other EZ-Fly routes are as shown.

From	To	Number of seats
Glasgow	Liverpool	12
Glasgow	Manchester	6
Liverpool	Manchester	4
Liverpool	Luton	6
Manchester	Luton	8

Formulate and solve a maximum flow problem to determine how many passengers can be re-routed from Glasgow to Luton on EZ-Fly flights.

8* (a) Find the range of possible values of the flow in arc DB in this network of upper and lower capacities.

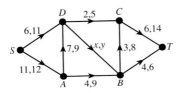

(b) Hence find the ranges of possible values of x and y.

9 The daily capacities, in 1000s of people, of a national network of coaches are shown in the table.

		To				
		London	Birmingham	Manchester	Leeds	Edinburgh
	London	–	30	–	20	–
	Birmingham	–	–	20	10	–
From	Manchester	–	–	–	10	15
	Leeds	–	–	–	–	25
	Edinburgh	–	–	–	–	–

(a) What is the maximum number of people per day who can use this company to travel from London to Edinburgh?

(b) Find a minimum cut for the underlying network.

Miscellaneous exercise 2

1 The diagram represents a system of pipes.
   The weights show the (directed) maximum
   capacity for each pipe in litres per minute.

   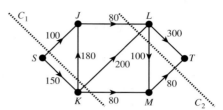

   (a) Calculate the values of the cuts C_1 and C_2
       marked in the diagram.

   (b) Explain what the values calculated in part (a)
       tell you about the maximum flow
       from S to T.

   (OCR)

2 The diagrams show the maximum capacities of the arcs in a directed distribution network,
   and the flows currently established in the network.

   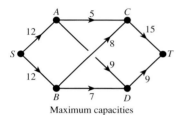
   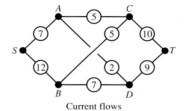

   Maximum capacities   Current flows

   (a) Find a minimum cut and give its capacity.

   (b) Say why the established flows do not give a maximum total flow through the network.

   (c) Use the labelling procedure to find a set of flows which do produce a maximum flow
       through the network.   (AQA, adapted)

3 The figure shows a system of pipes with the lower
   and upper capacities, in litres per second, for each
   pipe.

   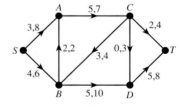

   (a) Draw a diagram showing a flow from S to T of
       7 litres per second.

   (b) Augment your solution to part (a), using the
       labelling procedure and showing your working
       clearly, to find the maximum flow from S
       to T.   (OCR)

4 The figure shows a system of pipes and the upper and
   lower capacities of each pipe, in litres per second.

   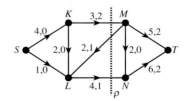

   (a) Work out the capacity of the cut ρ marked on
       the diagram.

   (b) Describe a flow from S to T with value 2 less than
       the capacity of the cut ρ.

   (c) What can you deduce from the results of parts (a)
       and (b)?   (OCR)

5 The diagram shows a network of pathways in a maze. Rats move steadily through the maze.

Node S represents the entrance and node T represents the exit. The weights on the arcs show the maximum number of rats per minute that can move along each pathway.

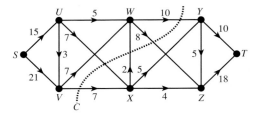

(a) Obtain the value of the cut marked C on the diagram.

(b) What can you deduce from your answer to part (a) about the flow of rats through the maze?

(c) Use a labelling procedure to construct a flow of 23 rats per minute.

(d) Write down the arcs that are saturated in your answer to part (c). What can you deduce from this about the flow of rats through the maze. Explain your reasoning.   (OCR, adapted)

6 The linear programme below is to find a maximum flow from S to T in the network shown. The numbers show the maximum allowable flows along the arcs.

Flows that are established along arcs are indicated by x-values. For instance, the value of x_{SA} gives the flow along the arc SA.

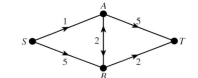

A computer package is used to solve the linear programme.

Maximise $F = x_{SA} + x_{SB}$
subject to $x_{SA} + x_{BA} - x_{AT} - x_{AB} = 0,$
$x_{SB} + x_{AB} - x_{BA} - x_{BT} = 0,$
$x_{SA} \leqslant 1, \quad x_{AT} \leqslant 5, \quad x_{AB} \leqslant 2,$
$x_{BA} \leqslant 2, \quad x_{SB} \leqslant 5, \quad x_{BT} \leqslant 2,$
all x-values $\geqslant 0.$

The solution given by the computer package is

F	x_{SA}	x_{SB}	x_{AB}	x_{BA}	x_{AT}	x_{BT}
5	1	4	0	2	3	2

(a) What maximum flow is given by this solution? Give a cut to prove that this flow is a maximum flow. Say why your cut proves that the flow is maximal.

(b) The two equality constraints refer to nodes A and B respectively. Explain briefly the purpose of the equality constraints.

(c) Explain the structure of the objective function, and give an alternative objective function.   (AQA, adapted)

7 The figure shows a system of motorways and the maximum capacities, in thousands of vehicles per hour, on each motorway.

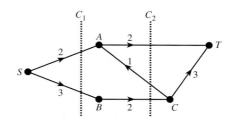

(a) Calculate the values of the cuts C_1 and C_2.

(b) Copy and complete the table below, showing every possible cut and its capacity.

Arcs in cut	Nodes on source side	Nodes on sink side	Capacity of cut
SA, SB	S	A, B, C, T	
SA, BC	S, B	A, C, T	

(c) State the maximum flow from S to T.   (OCR)

8 The figure shows a system of corridors and the maximum number of people who can move along the corridor (in either direction) each minute. When the fire bell rings all the people in the three rooms S_1, S_2 and S_3 must move along the corridors to one of the two fire assembly points T_1 or T_2.

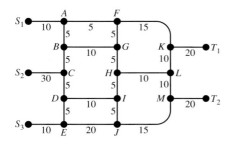

(a) Show how the network can be modified so that it has a single source, S, and a single sink, T. (You need not redraw the whole network.)

(b) A cut, γ, separates the nodes of the figure into the two sets X and Y, where $X = \{S_1, S_2, S_3, A, B, C, D\}$ and $Y = \{E, F, G, H, I, J, K, L, M, T_1, T_2\}$. Ignoring the rest of the network, calculate the maximum number of people per minute who can cross γ from X to Y.

(c) Give a flow in which exactly 25 people per minute move from S to T.

(d) (i) Find the maximum number of people per minute who can move from S to T.

(ii) Use the maximum flow–minimum cut theorem to show that the flow in (i) is maximal.   (OCR)

9 The figure shows a system of telephone cables and the maximum number of telephone lines, in thousands, that each cable can carry.

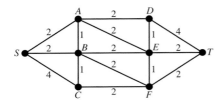

(a) Draw a diagram showing how S and T can be joined by five thousand lines.

(b) Augment your answer to part (a), using a labelling procedure and showing your working clearly, to find the maximum number of lines that the system can carry between S and T.

(c) Use the maximum flow–minimum cut theorem to verify that your answer found in part (b) is maximal.   (OCR)

10 The figure shows a network of directed arcs. The values on the arcs show the maximum and minimum capacities, in litres per second.

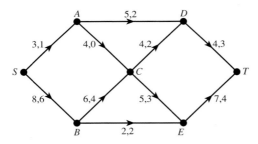

(a) The flow through node C must be at least 5 litres per second. Explain how to modify the network to show this, using directed arcs with maximum and minimum capacities.

(b) A cut, γ, separates the nodes into the two sets $\{S, A, B, D\}$ and $\{C, E, T\}$. Calculate the maximum possible flow across γ.

(c) Explain what the value calculated in part (b) tells you about the maximum flow through the network.   (OCR)

3 Critical path analysis

This chapter is about scheduling large projects. When you have completed it you should

- know how to construct and interpret activity networks
- be able to find earliest and latest start times by performing forward and reverse passes
- be able to identify critical activities and find a critical path
- know how to construct and interpret cascade charts and resource histograms
- understand how to carry out resource levelling.

3.1 Activity networks

Figure 3.1 represents just one part of the process followed by the Sainsbury supermarket chain when launching a new product.

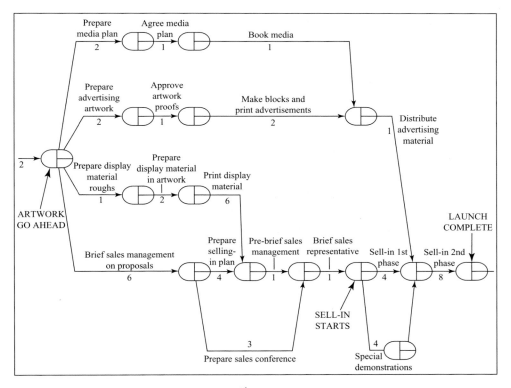

Fig. 3.1

This diagram is an example of an **activity network**. Such networks are useful because they express a project in a form which is visually meaningful, indicating, for example, which tasks must be done in sequence and which can be done at the same time. More importantly, activity networks allow questions of scheduling and resource use to be tackled systematically, using **critical path analysis**.

The techniques of critical path analysis were developed in the late 1950s by the US Navy and DuPont to plan and monitor such large-scale projects as the Polaris missile programme. Their general aim is to determine the minimum time in which a project can be completed and to optimise the use of manpower and resources in achieving this minimum completion time.

The starting point of critical path analysis is to break a project down into individual activities and to draw up a table showing the duration of each activity and which activities must be completed before a given activity can be started.

Consider a simple decorating project which involves the activities shown in Table 3.2.

Activity	Duration (hours)	Immediately preceding activities
A Prepare walls and ceiling	2	–
B Sand woodwork	1	–
C Prepare floor	1	–
D Paint woodwork	2	A, B
E Allow paint to dry	8	D
F Emulsion walls and ceiling	3	E
G Lay new flooring	2	C, F
H Construct shelving unit	3	–
I Fix unit	1	H, F

Table 3.2

When constructing an activity network, it is conventional to let the arcs of the network represent the activities. The nodes are drawn as circles to leave space for numbers which will be explained in the next section.

The network should be drawn so that preceding activities are all shown to the left of the given activity. For example, D is preceded by A and B so you should draw A and B to the left of D, as in Fig. 3.3.

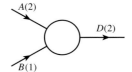

The numbers in the brackets indicate the durations of the activities.

Fig. 3.3

> Note that some textbooks use the alternative convention of letting the nodes represent the activities.

The situation involving G and I is more complicated. Activities C and F precede G, whereas H and F precede I.

You might be tempted to draw a diagram like that in Fig. 3.4, but Fig. 3.4 implies that C, F and H all precede G and I, and this is not true. Figure 3.4 *is incorrect*.

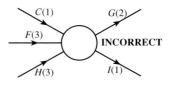

Fig. 3.4

The correct way to handle such situations is to introduce extra activities, called **dummy activities**, of zero duration. These dummy activities are indicated by the dotted lines in Fig. 3.5.

There is no need to name these activities, and as their duration is 0, this is not shown in the diagram either.

The whole activity network representing the project in Table 3.2 is shown in Fig. 3.6.

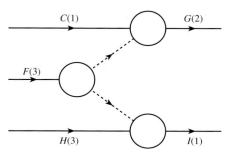

Fig. 3.5

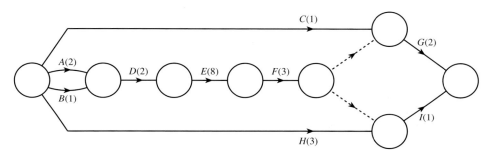

Fig. 3.6

Activity networks such as this are much easier to understand if you arrange them so that an activity which follows another is always to its right.

Procedure for drawing an activity network

Step 1 Draw a circle to represent the start of all those activities that have no immediate predecessors.

Step 2 From the most recently drawn circles draw the start of arcs directed from left to right to represent the activities starting from those circles.

Step 3 To the right of any previous drawing, draw circles to represent the start of all those activities for which all predecessors have already been drawn. Two activities which have precisely the same immediate predecessors can share a start circle.

Step 4 Join all loose arcs to relevant right-hand circles, introducing dummy activities as necessary.

Step 5 Repeat Steps 2, 3 and 4 until all activities have been considered.

Step 6 Join all loose arcs to a circle at the right-hand side of the diagram, to represent the finish.

In practice, computers are used to draw activity networks, and to carry out the optimisation processes.

3.2   Earliest and latest starting times

An important aspect of critical path analysis is determining the possible starting and finishing times of activities. The earliest time after the start of a project that an activity can be started is called the **earliest start time**, or the **early time**.

It is useful to adopt a standard notation for labelling the nodes with times. Draw a line down the centre of the circle representing the node. The early time for activities leading out of the node is placed on the left side of this line, as in Fig. 3.7.

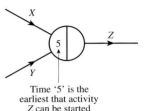

Time '5' is the earliest that activity Z can be started

Fig. 3.7

The early times are calculated by performing a **forward pass**; that is working through the activity network, from left to right, according to the early time algorithm.

> **Early time algorithm (forward pass)**
>
> **Step 1**   Label the initial node with early time 0.
>
> **Step 2**   Choose any node, X say, such that all nodes to its left have already been given an early time.
>
> **Step 3**   Consider all activities leading into X, and the nodes from which they come. Label X with an early time equal to the maximum value of early time of preceding node + duration of preceding activity for all these activities.
>
> **Step 4**   If all nodes have been labelled then stop. Otherwise, return to Step 2.

Example 3.2.1
Find the early time for node X in the activity network shown in the diagram.

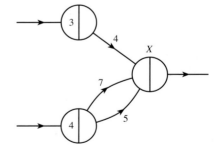

Three activities lead into X. The early time for X is therefore the maximum of

$$3 + 4, \quad 4 + 7, \quad 4 + 5.$$

The maximum of these is 11, so the early time is 11.

Note that the early time algorithm is really just common sense. How early you can start an activity depends on how soon the tasks on which it depends can be completed. In Example 3.2.1, any activities following node X cannot start until 7 units of time after time 4. The earliest start time for any such activity must therefore be 11.

Example 3.2.2
When is the earliest that the project shown in the
activity network on the right can be completed?

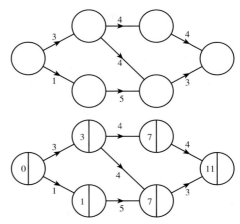

Applying the early time algorithm gives
the early times shown in the second
diagram.

The earliest time the project can be
completed is shown in the right-most
node, which is 11.

The **late time** for a node is the latest that
activities to the left can finish and still not delay
the completion of the project.

Once you have determined all the early times you can
calculate the late times by performing a **reverse pass**, that is working back through the
network from right to left, according to the late time algorithm. The late times are written on
the right side of the node.

> **Late time algorithm (reverse pass)**
>
> **Step 1** Label the final node with a late time equal to its early time.
>
> **Step 2** Choose any node, X say, such that all nodes to its right have
> already been given a late time.
>
> **Step 3** Consider all activities leading out of X. Label X with a late time
> equal to the least value of
>
> late time of following node – duration of following activity
> for all these activities.
>
> **Step 4** If all nodes have been labelled then stop. Otherwise, return to
> Step 2.

Example 3.2.3
Find the late time for node X.

Three activities lead out of X. The late time
for X is therefore the least of

$$9 - 3, \quad 8 - 4, \quad 14 - 7.$$

The least of these is 4, so the late time for
node X is 4.

Once again, the application of the algorithm should be common
sense. How late you can start an activity depends on how much time is
available, and what else must be done, before the completion of the project.

Example 3.2.4

Complete the early and late times for Example 3.2.2.

Applying the late time algorithm to the solution of Example 3.2.2 gives the solution below.

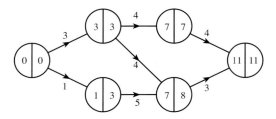

A simple check on your working is to ensure that, when you have finished, the initial node has times 0, 0.

The early and late times for the nodes refer to the totality of activities leading into and out of the nodes. It is straightforward to use these to determine the earliest and latest times for individual activities.

Example 3.2.5

Part of a network is shown in the diagram. Determine the earliest and latest start and finish times for activity A.

The earliest start time for activity A is the same as the early time for its left-hand node, that is 4. The earliest finish time is therefore $4 + 2 = 6$.

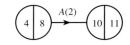

The latest finish time for A is the same as the late time for its right-hand node, that is 11. The latest start time is therefore $11 - 2 = 9$.

Exercise 3A

1 Draw activity networks for the projects with activities as given in the tables.

(a)

Activity	Duration	Immediately preceding activities
A	4	—
B	8	—
C	9	A
D	3	B
E	6	C
F	2	C, D
G	5	F

(b)

Activity	Duration (min)	Immediately preceding activities
A Pre-heat oven	10	–
B Grease tin	0.5	–
C Cream fat and sugar	2	–
D Beat in eggs	0.5	C
E Fold in flour	1	D
F Put mixture in tin	0.5	B, E
G Bake cake	10	A, F

2 Complete the early and late times for this activity network.

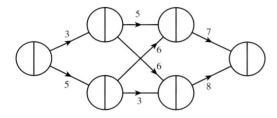

3 Complete the early and late times for the activity networks described in Question 1(a) and 1(b).

4 Find the earliest possible completion time for the project with activity network as shown.

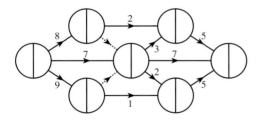

5 Four activities, their expected durations and precedences are shown in the table.

(a) Draw an activity network to represent these activities and their precedences.

(b) Determine the earliest and latest starting time for each activity, for completion of the project in the minimum time.

Activity	Duration	Immediately preceding activities
A	3	–
B	2	–
C	1	A, B
D	4	A, B

6 A construction project is divided into nine activities as shown.

(a) Construct an activity network for the project.

(b) Determine the earliest and latest starting times for each activity.

Activity	Duration (weeks)	Immediate predecessors
A	2	—
B	2	—
C	1	A
D	2	A, B
E	3	B
F	1	C
G	4	C, D, E
H	3	E
I	3	F, G, H

3.3 Critical activities

Consider again the activity network from Example 3.2.4, which is shown in Fig. 3.8.

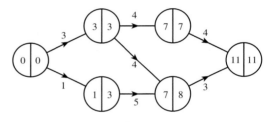

Fig. 3.8

The activity of duration 5 can start as early as time 1 and must finish by time 8. This information is illustrated in Fig. 3.9, where the shaded rectangles show the earliest and latest possible periods during which the activity takes place.

For this activity the two periods are not the same. There is therefore flexibility in the scheduling of this task. The technical term for this flexibility in scheduling is **float**.

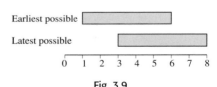

Fig. 3.9

However, other activities have no such flexibility. They are called critical activities because their prompt completion is critical to whether or not the project can be carried out in the least possible time.

Once you have determined the early and late times, you can easily pick out critical activities because

- they connect two nodes where both nodes have the same early and late times,
- their duration is the difference between the labels of their left and right nodes.

An example is the activity at the top of Fig. 3.8, shown isolated
in Fig. 3.10.

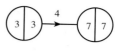

Fig. 3.10

> A **critical activity** is an activity for which there is no scheduling
> flexibility.

Since the successful completion of critical activities is essential to the prompt completion of
the entire project, these are the activities which must be monitored most closely and to which
manpower and machinery must be reallocated if there are any snags.

Each activity network has at least one path of critical activities leading from the start node to
the final node. This path is called the **critical path**.

An example of a critical path for the activity network in Fig. 3.8 is shown by the thick path in
Fig. 3.11.

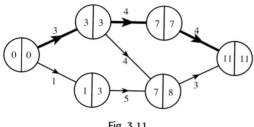

Fig. 3.11

> A **critical path** is a path of critical activities leading from the start node
> to the final node.

Exercise 3B

1 What is the critical path for the network shown in the diagram?

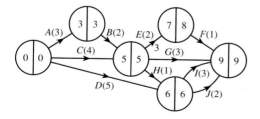

2 Suppose that for the network in Question 1 just one of activities *E, G, I* and *J* can be speeded
up. Which one would you choose to accelerate? Explain your answer.

3 Complete the early and late times for the network shown when the duration of activity X is

(a) $t = 4$,

(b) $t = 2$.

For what range of values of t is activity X critical?

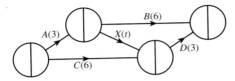

4 Henry and Lucinda are organising a children's party for their young daughter Abigail. The table lists the activities involved, their expected durations and precedences.

	Activity	Duration (days)	Preceded by
A	Decide who to invite	2	–
B	Find a suitable room and book it	5	–
C	Send out invitations and get replies	8	A, B
D	Book entertainment	3	B
E	Book caterer	2	C
F	Buy party bags	1	C
G	Buy Abigail a new party dress	3	D

(a) Draw an activity network to represent these activities and their precedences.

(b) Determine the earliest and latest starting time for each activity, for completion of the party arrangements in the minimum time.

(c) Identify the critical path and find the minimum time for completion of the party arrangements.

Lucinda and Henry find that the replies all come much sooner than they had expected, and so although they had allowed eight days for activity C it only takes three days.

(d) Identify the critical path assuming that activity C only takes three days.   (OCR)

5 The table gives details of five tasks which have to be completed to finish a project.

(a) Produce an activity network for the project.

(b) Perform a forward pass and a backward pass to find the minimum time to completion and the critical tasks.

Activity	Duration	Immediate predecessors
A	5	–
B	2	–
C	1	B
D	2	A, B
E	3	A, C

6 (a) Draw an activity network for the project whose activities are described in the table.

Activity	Duration (weeks)	Immediate predecessors
A	2	–
B	4	–
C	1	A, B
D	3	B
E	6	C
F	1	C, D
G	2	D

(b) Use an appropriate algorithm to find the critical path and the minimum completion time.

(c) Which activity can have its start time delayed by the greatest possible time without affecting the overall completion time?

7 A project has the activity network shown. The times are given in days.

(a) Determine the critical path and project duration.

(b) By how much will the project be delayed if the duration of each activity is increased by two days?

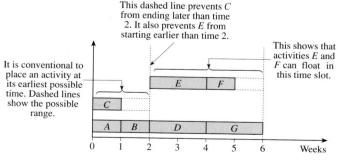

3.4   Cascade charts

Once the early and late times have been calculated, a cascade chart provides a good way of displaying the information in a way which is easy to understand. Figure 3.12 is an example of a cascade chart.

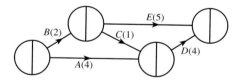

Fig. 3.12

You can easily spot the following features of this project.

- The project can be completed in a minimum of six weeks.
- Activities A, B, D and G cannot 'float', and are therefore critical.
- Activity C precedes D, and can start at any time during the first week.
- Activity E precedes F and can start at any time during the third week.

When constructing a cascade chart it is a good idea to deal first with all the critical activities since their time slots are completely fixed.

Example 3.4.1

Construct a cascade chart for a project with the activities given in the table.

Activity	Duration (weeks)	Immediate predecessors
A	5	–
B	3	–
C	2	–
D	3	A, B
E	4	B, C

Start by constructing an activity network with the early and late times. This is shown on the next page.

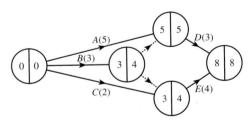

From the activity network, you can see that the critical path is A, D, so start the cascade chart by putting these across the bottom of the chart.

Then note that the earliest start times of B and C are both zero, so this allows you to place them at the left of the diagram.

Finally, E can float between 3 and 8, and is placed at its earliest possible time, which is 3.

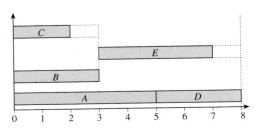

3.5   Resource levelling

So far, you have only been concerned with the time scale of activities and not what resources are needed. For example, the number of people needed for each task has not been considered. For most applications the availability and costs of resources are just as vital as the time scale. A first step in dealing with these issues is to draw a **resource histogram**.

Consider, for example, Fig. 3.13 which shows the cascade chart for a project and notes the resources required for the various activities.

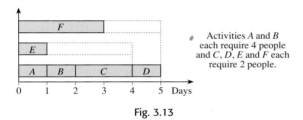

Activities A and B each require 4 people and C, D, E and F each require 2 people.

Fig. 3.13

The numbers of people required for each day are then shown in the resource histogram in Fig. 3.14.

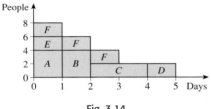

Fig. 3.14

For some businesses, it may be appropriate to use resources in this way, with more people needed at the beginning of the project. However, for many applications it is better to even out the use of resources as much as possible. For example, small construction firms will often employ a number of full-time staff. It is important that these staff are always fully employed rather than doing nothing. Most firms would want to avoid employing temporary labour if at all possible.

The smoothing out of the usage of resources is called **resource levelling.** For the project shown in Fig. 3.14, resource levelling can be achieved as shown in Fig. 3.15, with the new resource histogram shown in Fig. 3.16.

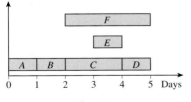

Fig. 3.15

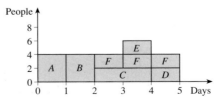

Fig. 3.16

Example 3.5.1

For the project with activities as shown, use resource levelling to find a schedule and an allocation of personnel which enables the project to be completed as soon as possible, but using at most three people at any one time.

Activity	Duration (days)	People needed	Immediate predecessors
A	2	2	–
B	4	1	–
C	1	2	–
D	3	1	C
E	1	1	A
F	1	1	B, D
G	3	2	B, E

Start by drawing the activity network and identifying the critical path, which is B, G.

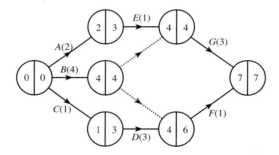

Then draw the cascade chart, starting along the bottom with the critical path.

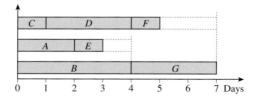

From the cascade chart, you can see that activities A and C can be done in either order. A possible resource histogram is shown on the right.

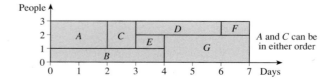

Exercise 3C

1 The network represents the activities involved in a project and their durations in hours.

(a) Perform a critical path analysis to find the minimum project completion time and the critical activities.

(b) Construct a cascade chart for the project, assuming each activity is to start as early as possible.

(c) Assuming that each activity requires one person, state the maximum number of people required for the schedule of part (b). How can the project be completed in the minimum time but using at most two people at any one time?

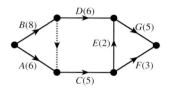

2 The table shows the activities involved in a project, their durations, their immediate predecessors, and the number of people needed for each activity.

Activity	A	B	C	D	E	F
Duration (days)	1	2	1	1	4	2
Immediate predecessors	–	–	A, B	B	B	C, D
People needed	1	3	2	2	2	2

(a) Draw an activity network for this project.

(b) Perform forward and backward passes in order to find the critical path and the minimum project duration.

(c) Schedule the activities so that the project is completed as quickly as possible, using no more than four people at any one time. (AQA)

3 The activities involved in organising a charity event are shown in the activity network, where the durations are in days.

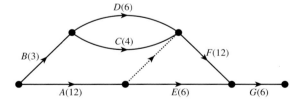

(a) Find the critical path and its duration. State the earliest and latest starting and finishing times for each activity.

(b) Given that each activity requires one helper in order to complete the project on time, find the minimum number of such helpers.

(c) The organiser has to cope with one fewer helper than required in part (b). Find the least possible delay to the completion of the project and state how this can be achieved.

4 A construction firm is involved in a building project subdivided into six major tasks as shown in the table.

Activity	Duration (days)	Workers needed	Immediate predecessors
A	14	2	–
B	6	1	–
C	4	3	B
D	10	3	A, C
E	20	1	B
F	16	4	B

(a) Assuming that enough workers are available, construct an activity network for the project. Find the critical path and the shortest possible finishing time for the building.

(b) Construct a resource histogram for the number of workers required, assuming that each task is to start as early as possible.

(c) Given that the firm employs eight full-time workers, describe how to schedule the activities so as to enable the earliest possible completion time without requiring the employment of additional workers.

Miscellaneous exercise 3

1 The table gives details of a set of six tasks which have to be completed to finish a project. The 'immediate predecessors' are those tasks which must be completed before a task may be started.

Task	Duration (days)	Immediate predecessors
A	2	–
B	8	–
C	5	A
D	4	A
E	2	A, B
F	2	B, C, D

(a) Produce an activity network for the project.

(b) Perform a forward pass and a backward pass to find the minimum time for completion and the critical tasks.

The following table shows, for each task, the extra cost that would be incurred in using extra resources to complete the task in one day less than the normal duration.

Task	A	B	C	D	E	F
Extra cost (£), for completion in 1 day less	1000	1250	750	500	1000	1000

(c) Find the minimum extra cost to complete the project in one day less than the minimum completion time which you found in part (b).   (AQA)

2 The table lists six activities involved in painting a room.

	Activity	Duration (hours)	Preceded by
A	Prepare walls etc.	5	—
B	Undercoat walls	2	A
C	Paint ceiling	1	A
D	Paint walls	2	B, C
E	Paint woodwork	4	B, C
F	Tidy up	1	D, E

(a) Draw an activity network to represent these activities and their precedences.

(b) Determine the earliest and latest starting time for each activity.

(c) Identify the critical path, and the minimum time for completion of the painting, from start to finish, assuming that there is sufficient manpower available.

A start lag of 1 hour is to be incorporated between activities B and E.

(d) Describe what the start lag represents in relation to the activities B and E, and the effect that it will have on the critical path.   (OCR)

3 A building project has been divided into a number of activities as shown in the table.

	Activity	Immediate predecessors	Duration (days)
A	Prepare site	—	1
B	Erect walls	A	4
C	Excavate and lay drains	A	7
D	Fit window frames	B	3
E	Erect roof	B	9
F	Install electrics	B	7
G	Install plumbing	C, D	6
H	Insulate roof	E	3
I	Plaster walls	F, G, H	2

(a) Construct an activity network for the project.

(b) Find the earliest start time for each activity for completion in the minimum time.

(c) Find the latest finish time for each activity for completion in the minimum time.

(d) Identify the critical path and state the shortest completion time for the whole project.

(e) Construct a cascade diagram for the project, assuming each activity is to start as early as possible.

(f) Each activity requires one worker. Draw a resource histogram showing the number of workers required each day.

(g) Given that there are only three workers available on any day, show how the activities could be allocated so that the project may be finished in the shortest completion time.   (AQA, adapted)

4 A major construction project is to be
undertaken and the project has been
divided into 11 activities, as shown in
the table.

(a) Construct an activity network for
the project.

(b) Find the earliest start time for each
activity.

(c) Find the latest finish time for each
activity.

(d) Identify the critical path and state
the shortest completion time for the
whole project.

Activity	Immediate predecessors	Duration (weeks)
A	–	3
B	–	4
C	A	2
D	B	3
E	C, D	5
F	C	6
G	D	7
H	E, F, G	4
I	G	6
J	F	8
K	H, I, J	3

Some of the activities can be speeded up at an additional cost. The following table lists the
activities that can be speeded up, their additional cost in £ per week, together with the
minimum times required to complete the activities.

Activity	Additional cost (£ per week)	Minimum time (weeks)
E	5000	1
I	4000	4
J	3000	5

The company wants to complete the project as soon as possible.

(e) (i) Find which activities should be speeded up. For each such activity, state, with
justification, the reduction in the number of weeks.

(ii) Hence state the revised minimum time for the completion of the whole project.

(iii) Calculate the total additional cost the company would incur in meeting this revised
completion time.   (AQA)

5 The table at the top of the next page details the tasks, procedures and times associated with
a project. The project is complete when all tasks are completed.

(a) Draw an activity network for this project.

(b) Determine the earliest start time and latest start time for the tasks, for completion in
minimum time.

(c) Use your table from part (b) to identify the slack time available for each task. Hence,
write down the critical path and the minimum time to complete the project.   (OCR)

Task	Preceded by	Time, in days, to complete task
A	–	7
B	–	5
C	A	6
D	A	4
E	B	5
F	B	7
G	E	4
H	F	6
I	C, D	9
J	G, H, I	3

6 The production of a leaflet to advertise a swimming pool involves 11 activities, as shown in the table.

	Activity	Duration (days)	Preceded by
A	Rough plan	3	–
B	Get finance	6	A
C	Detailed plan	5	A
D	Take photographs	4	B, C
E	Write text	6	B, C
F	Edit copy	2	D, E
G	Send to printer	1	F
H	Canvass likely interest	3	F
I	Check print proofs	1	G
J	Have leaflets printed	6	H, I
K	Send out leaflets	1	J

(a) Draw an activity network to illustrate these activities and their precedences.

(b) Determine the earliest and latest start times for each activity.

(c) Identify the critical path and the minimum time for completion for the production of the leaflets, from start to finish.

(d) The production team realise that they can begin to canvass likely interest (activity *H*) before editing copy (activity *F*) is completed. Explain briefly how this will alter the critical path and the minimum time for completion.   (OCR)

7 The table lists six activities in a project, together with their durations, precedences and the number of people required for each activity.

Activity	Duration (days)	Preceded by	People required
A	3	–	2
B	2	–	3
C	1	A, B	2
D	5	B	4
E	4	C	2
F	5	D, E	1

In addition to the precedences shown in the table, activity E must not start until at least four days after activity B has started.

(a) Draw an activity network to represent these activities and their precedences.

(b) Determine the earliest and latest starting times for each activity, for completion of the project in the minimum time.

(c) Identify the critical activities, and the minimum time for completion of the project, assuming that there are sufficient people available.

(d) Find the minimum number of people required at any given time to complete the project in the minimum time. Explain your reasoning carefully.   (OCR)

8 The table lists nine activities involved in building an attic extension, their durations and precedences.

	Activity	Duration (days)	Preceded by
A	Draw up plans and get planning permission	45	–
B	Clear rubbish and prepare site	16	–
C	Order stairs and window frames	12	A
D	Build new entrance and fit stairs	2	B, C
E	Install electrics	4	A, B
F	Fit floor	3	D, E
G	Fit window	1	D
H	Plaster walls	1	G, F
I	Decorate	3	H

(a) Draw an activity network to represent these activities and their precedences.

(b) Determine the earliest and latest starting times for each activity, for completion of the extension in the minimum possible time.

(c) Identify the critical path, and the minimum time for completion of the extension.

To save time, activity C (order stairs and window frames) is brought forward so that it happens at the same time as activity A.

(d) Work out how many days this will save on the whole project.   (OCR)

9 The table lists activities which form a project, with their durations and precedences.

Activity	Duration (min)	Preceded by
A	5	—
B	2	A
C	4	A
D	5	B
E	4	B, C
F	3	C
G	2	D, E
H	3	E, F
I	4	G, H

(a) Draw an activity network to represent the project.

(b) Determine the earliest and latest starting time for each activity, for completion of the project in the minimum possible time.

(c) Identify the critical path, and the minimum time for completion of the project. (OCR)

10 Paul is preparing a meal for his girlfriend. The table lists the activities involved, together with their durations and precedences.

	Activity	Duration (min)	Preceded by
A	Prepare table	5	—
B	Chop vegetables	8	—
C	Mix spices	5	—
D	Cook rice	20	—
E	Cook curry	10	B, C
F	Serve chutneys	2	A
G	Cook poppadoms	5	F
H	Put food on plates	2	D, E, G

(a) Draw an activity network to represent the preparation of the meal.

(b) Assuming that Paul can carry out two or more activities simultaneously, use a forward pass to determine the minimum time for preparing the meal.

(c) Use a backwards pass to identify the critical activities for preparing the meal in the minimum time, with the assumption from part (b).

Activities D, E and G may be carried out simultaneously, and activity D may be carried out at the same time as any activity except activity H. Otherwise Paul cannot carry out more than one activity at a time.

(d) Calculate the minimum time for the preparation of the meal under these conditions.
   (*You do not have to use a cascade chart, but you may do so if you wish.*)   (OCR)

4 Dynamic programming

This chapter looks at a method of analysing optimisation problems involving sequences of decisions. When you have completed it you should

- understand the idea of working backwards with sub-optimisation
- know what is meant by stage and state variables, actions and costs and be able to use these ideas
- know how to set up dynamic programming tabulations
- be able to use dynamic programming tabulations to solve minimising, maximising, minimax and maximin problems.

4.1 Various optimisation problems

Mathematicians always look for unifying ideas in their work. You can see broad examples of this unification by considering the different areas of mathematics. Mechanics is unified by the ideas of force and motion, and calculus by the use of limiting processes. You can also find more particular examples of unification within a single area of mathematics. Network diagrams are a unifying idea within discrete mathematics.

A directed network such as the one in Fig. 4.1 can model a variety of different types of problem. Here are some examples.

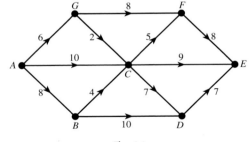

Fig. 4.1

1 The weights on the arcs are distances in miles. Find the shortest route from A to E.

2 Each weight represents the weight limit of vehicles, in tonnes, that can travel on that section of road. What is the heaviest vehicle that can travel from A to E?

3 The weights represent profits in £1000s which can be made by carrying cargo en route from A to E. Find the maximum possible profit for a journey from A to E.

4 The weights represent the times in hours needed to walk between campsites. Find a route from A to E which keeps the longest stretch to a minimum.

5 The weights represent activity durations in days. Find a critical path and the time necessary for completion of the entire project.

- Problem 1 is a **minimising** problem, finding a shortest route, for which you already know an algorithm, namely Dijkstra's algorithm (see D1 Section 4.2).
- Problem 5 is a critical path problem for which you already know an algorithm. In fact Problems 5 and 3 are actually solved the same way! They are both **maximising** problems involving finding a longest route.
- Problems 2 and 4 are new types of optimising problems.

In fact, all of these problems can be solved by one general method called **dynamic programming**. This is a term coined by Richard Bellman to describe techniques he and others developed in the 1950s to study optimisation problems involving sequences of decisions to be made by managers.

4.2   Terminology

Dynamic programming employs certain terminology which will be illustrated by the network of Fig. 4.2.

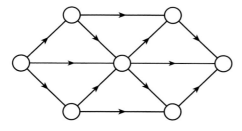

Fig. 4.2

The nodes are called **states**, the directed arcs are called **actions** and the weight on an arc is called the **cost**.

> An action is what transforms a situation from one state to another.

If you look at Fig. 4.2, you can see that one state requires 4 actions before reaching the final state, two require 3 actions, one requires 2 actions, and so on. The final state requires 0 actions to get to the final state. The maximum number of actions to get from a state to the final state is called the **stage variable**. Figure 4.3 shows the stage variables for each state.

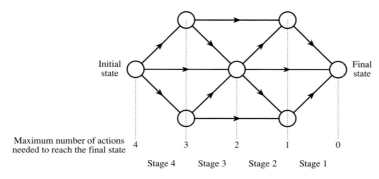

Fig. 4.3

The transition from a state to another whose stage variable is one less is called a **stage.** More specifically, the transition from states with stage variable k to states with stage variable $k - 1$ is called Stage k. This is shown in Fig. 4.3.

> Notice that the transition from a state with stage variable 4 to one with stage variable 2 is not a stage. Note also the importance of the word 'maximum' in the definition of stage variable. In Fig. 4.3, it is possible to get from the initial state to the final state with 2 actions, but the stage variable is 4 because this is the *maximum* number of actions required.

In addition to the stage variable, you can define a state variable for each state. For all the states with the same value of the stage variable the **state variable** is the number of the state as you move down the diagram from top to bottom.

Each state can thus be labelled with a pair of numbers: (stage variable, state variable). Figure 4.4 shows the labels for Fig. 4.3.

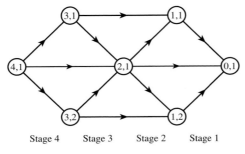

Fig. 4.4

Thus the labelling of a state as (3, 2) shows that

- the maximum possible number of actions to move to the final state is 3,
- this is the second such state moving down the diagram from top to bottom.

Example 4.2.1
Label the states of Fig. 4.5a.

The solution is shown in Fig. 4.5b.

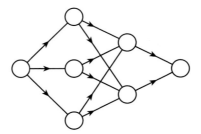

Fig. 4.5a

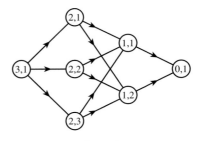

Fig. 4.5b

4.3   Minimising and maximising problems

Richard Bellman realised that a simple, general strategy can be used to solve optimisation problems involving a sequence of decisions. The principle of his method is that you should work backwards through the decisions, at each stage working out the best strategy from that point.

In this section you will see how to apply this idea to problems which require finding maxima or minima. The idea, when stated in a general way, is called Bellman's optimising principle.

> To solve an optimising problem involving a sequence of decisions you can work backwards. At each stage you should work out the best strategy from that point, called the **sub-optimal strategy**.

Suppose that to meet an increased demand for electricity in a town, it is intended to increase the capacity of parts of the electricity grid on one route from the generator to the town. The costs, in £10,000s, of bringing each part of the grid up to maximum capacity are shown in Fig. 4.6.

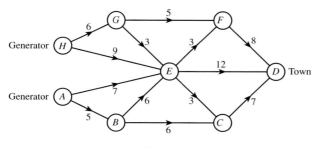

Fig. 4.6

To use dynamic programming to find the cheapest way of upgrading the grid, first label the states in the standard way. This gives

$$D(0, 1), \quad F(1, 1), \quad C(1, 2), \quad E(2, 1), \quad G(3, 1), \quad B(3, 2), \quad H(4, 1), \quad A(4, 2).$$

Similarly, number the actions from each state from top to bottom. Thus, focusing for the moment on state E, the actions EF, ED and EC are numbered 1, 2 and 3 respectively.

Alternatively, each action can be labelled by reference to the state to which it moves. For E, these labels would be $(1, 1)$, $(0, 1)$ and $(1, 2)$.

Labelling the states (nodes) and numbering the actions (arcs) in this way enables you to work systematically back through the network considering all possible courses of action. The working can be laid out in tabular form, as in Table 4.7. The work for two stages is shown, and a commentary follows the table.

Stage	State	Action	Value	Current minimum
1	$F(1, 1)$	1	8	← 8
	$C(1, 2)$	1	7	← 7
2	$E(2, 1)$	1	$3 + 8 = 11$	
		2	12	
		3	$3 + 7 = 10$	← 10

Table 4.7

The first two rows of Table 4.7 refer to Stage 1. During Stage 1, you know that it costs 8 to go from F to D, and 7 to go from C to D. As these are the only transitions from F and C to D, no choices need to be made; these are the minimum routes from F and C.

The next three rows refer to Stage 2; E is the only state with stage variable 2.

The first action from E is the transition to F. This route to D costs $3 + 8 = 11$.

The second action from E is the direct transition to D, which costs 12.

The third action from E is the transition to C. This route to D costs $3 + 7 = 10$.

The three routes from E to D cost 11, 12 and 10; the minimum is 10, so the value of 10 is used from now on for all routes through $E(2, 1)$. Thus the sub-optimal strategy from E is the route with value 10.

The dynamic programming process is continued in Table 4.8.

Stage	State	Action	Value	Current minimum
1	$F(1, 1)$	1	8	← 8
	$C(1, 2)$	1	7	← 7
2	$E(2, 1)$	1	$3 + 8 = 11$	
		2	12	
		3	$3 + 7 = 10$	← 10
3	$G(3, 1)$	1	$5 + 8 = 13$	← 13
		2	$3 + 10 = 13$	
	$B(3, 2)$	1	$6 + 10 = 16$	
		2	$6 + 7 = 13$	← 13
4	$H(4, 1)$	1	$6 + 13 = 19$	← 19
		2	$9 + 10 = 19$	
	$A(4, 2)$	1	$7 + 10 = 17$	← 17
		2	$5 + 13 = 18$	

Table 4.8

The first row of Stage 3 refers to the route from G via F. This gives the cost of the action GF, which is 5, plus the minimum cost from F, which is 8, making a total of $5 + 8 = 13$.

The second row of Stage 3 refers to the route from G via E. This gives the cost of the action GE, which is 3, plus the minimum cost from E, which is 10, making a total of $3 + 10 = 13$.

Stage 4 is completed in a similar way. Because it is the final stage, the process ends having found minimum costs of 19 and 17, representing £19,000 from H and £17,000 from A.

It is therefore better to increase the capacity from Generator A. Retracing the best actions, namely action 1 from $A(4, 2)$ to $E(2, 1)$, then action 3 from $E(2, 1)$ to $C(1, 2)$ and finally action 1 from $C(1, 2)$ to $D(0, 1)$, yields the route $AECD$.

You can solve a problem involving maximising in a very similar way.

Example 4.3.1
The table shows the tasks in a project. Use dynamic programming to find the critical path.

Activity	Duration (days)	Immediate predecessors
A	10	–
B	11	A
C	6	–
D	10	A
E	7	B, C
F	9	D
G	5	E, F
H	4	G
I	7	E, F

Although it is possible to go straight from this information into a dynamic programming table without drawing an activity network, it is a good idea to start by drawing the network, and labelling the nodes using the dynamic programming conventions, with the slight modification that the activities (actions) are labelled with letters rather than numbers. Note, however, that the method of dealing with these actions is still systematic. For each state you consider the actions from top to bottom as if they were numbered.

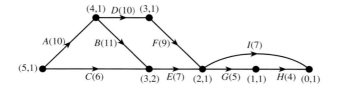

You are now in a position to set up the dynamic programming table.

Stage	State	Activity	Value	Current maximum
1	(1, 1)	H	4	← 4
2	(2, 1)	I	7	
		G	$5 + 4 = 9$	← 9
3	(3, 1)	F	$9 + 9 = 18$	← 18
	(3, 2)	E	$7 + 9 = 16$	← 16
4	(4, 1)	D	$10 + 18 = 28$	← 28
		B	$11 + 16 = 27$	
5	(5, 1)	A	$10 + 28 = 38$	← 38
		C	$6 + 16 = 22$	

The maximum duration, corresponding to the critical path, is 38 days. By retracing, the critical path is *ADFGH*.

Exercise 4A

1 Set up stage and state variables for the nodes of this diagram.

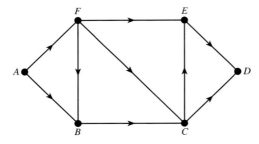

2 The various possible routes for a person commuting by car are as shown in the diagram. The weights represent the number of traffic lights per leg of the journey.

Use dynamic programming to find the route which minimises the number of traffic lights.

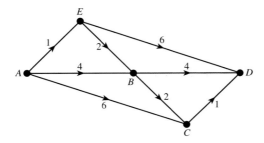

3 Set up and use dynamic programming tabulations to solve these two problems considered at the start of Section 4.1.

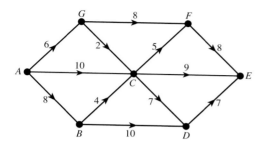

(a) Given that the arc weights represent distances in miles, find the shortest route from A to E.

(b) Given that the arc weights represent profits in £1000s which can be made by carrying cargo, find the maximum possible profit for a journey from A to E.

4 It is required to find the shortest route from A to D.

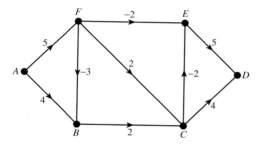

(a) Explain why Dijkstra's algorithm is not an appropriate method for this problem.

(b) Use dynamic programming to find the required route.

5 Set up and use a dynamic programming tabulation to find the longest paths from each of A, B and C to N.

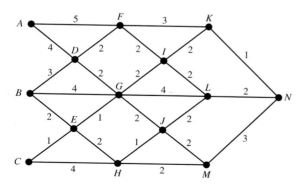

4.4   Maximin and minimax problems

The problems of Section 4.3 were maximising and minimising problems, but, going back to Section 4.1, problems 2 and 4, associated with the network of Fig. 4.1 were not simply questions of maximising or minimising. Problem 2 is reprinted here, as Example 4.4.1. Problem 4 is Example 4.4.2.

Example 4.4.1

In the diagram, each arc weight represents the weight limit on vehicles, in tonnes, that can travel on that section of road. What is the heaviest vehicle that can travel from A to E?

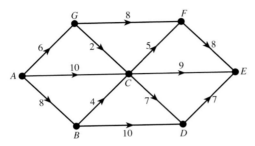

This problem is concerned primarily with the minimum weight limit which occurs on each of the routes from A to E. For example, the route $AGCFE$ has weight limits of 6, 2, 5 and 8 tonnes. So vehicles using this route are limited to 2 tonnes. To solve the problem it is necessary to find the route which maximises this minimum value. This is an example of a **maximin** problem.

The dynamic programming tabulation is started in the table below.

Stage	State	Action	Value	Current maximin
1	$F(1, 1)$	1	8	← 8
	$D(1, 2)$	1	7	← 7
2	$C(2, 1)$	1	$\min(5, 8) = 5$	
		2	9	← 9
		3	$\min(7, 7) = 7$	

In Stage 1, the maximum weights which can be carried from F and D respectively are 8 and 7 tonnes. In Stage 2 only state C must be considered. There are three routes from C to E. On each, the weight limit on the whole route is equal to the minimum of the limits on the individual sections. You can see that the sub-optimal route from C is the direct route to E, with weight limit 9; so the value of 9 is used from now on for all routes through C.

The process is continued in the table below.

Stage	State	Action	Value	Current maximin
1	$F(1, 1)$	1	8	$\leftarrow 8$
	$D(1, 2)$	1	7	$\leftarrow 7$
2	$C(2, 1)$	1	$\min(5, 8) = 5$	
		2	9	$\leftarrow 9$
		3	$\min(7, 7) = 7$	
3	$G(3, 1)$	1	$\min(8, 8) = 8$	$\leftarrow 8$
		2	$\min(2, 9) = 2$	
	$B(3, 2)$	1	$\min(4, 9) = 4$	
		2	$\min(10, 7) = 7$	$\leftarrow 7$
4	$A(4, 1)$	1	$\min(6, 8) = 6$	
		2	$\min(10, 9) = 9$	$\leftarrow 9$
		3	$\min(8, 7) = 7$	

The maximin, of 9 tonnes, is obtained by using the route ACE.

Example 4.4.2

In the figure, the arc weights represent the times in hours needed to walk between campsites. Find a route from A to E which keeps the longest leg to a minimum.

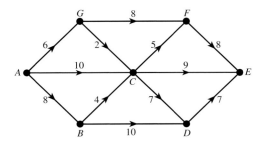

This problem is concerned primarily with the maximum time occurring on each of the routes from A to E. For example, the route $AGCFE$ has legs of length 6, 2, 5 and 8 hours. So the longest leg for walkers using this route is 8 hours. To solve this problem it is necessary to find the route which minimises this maximum value. This is an example of a **minimax** problem. The dynamic programming tabulation for this problem can be laid out as follows.

Stage	State	Action	Value	Current minimax
1	$F(1, 1)$	1	8	← 8
	$D(1, 2)$	1	7	← 7
2	$C(2, 1)$	1	$\max(5, 8) = 8$	
		2	9	
		3	$\max(7, 7) = 7$	← 7
3	$G(3, 1)$	1	$\max(8, 8) = 8$	
		2	$\max(2, 7) = 7$	← 7
	$B(3, 2)$	1	$\max(4, 7) = 7$	← 7
		2	$\max(10, 7) = 10$	
4	$A(4, 1)$	1	$\max(6, 7) = 7$	← 7
		2	$\max(10, 7) = 10$	
		3	$\max(8, 7) = 8$	

The minimax, of 7 hours, is obtained by using route *AGCDE*. This means that walkers using this route have a longest leg of only 7 hours.

Exercise 4B

1 Classify each of the following scenarios as being a maximising, a minimising, a maximin or a minimax problem.

   (a) The organisers of a trans-desert race wish to make the longest leg as short as possible to minimise the amount of water that needs to be carried.

   (b) A commuter wishes to travel on a route which involves the least number of traffic lights.

   (c) Another commuter wishes to travel on a route where the speed limits permit the minimum speed to be as large as possible.

   (d) For tax purposes, an author wishes to arrange payments from his publishers in such a way as to minimise his maximum annual income.

   (e) A production line has to be organised in such a way that the slowest stage is as fast as possible.

2 The diagram shows a network with (stage, state) variables at the nodes and costs on the arcs.

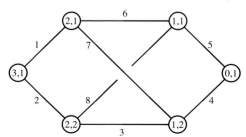

Find the following four routes:

(a) maximum,

(b) minimum,

(c) maximin,

(d) minimax.

In each case, complete a dynamic programming tabulation, showing stages, states and actions together with sub-optimal strategies.

3 The numbers on the arcs of this network represent the maximum weight (in tonnes) of a vehicle allowed on the road that the arc represents.

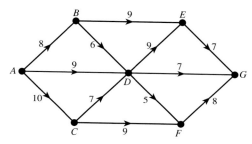

Use dynamic programming to find the heaviest vehicle that can travel from A to G.

4 The network represents a set of routes used by a cargo plane flying from A to E. The weights represent the duration, in hours, of legs of the flight.

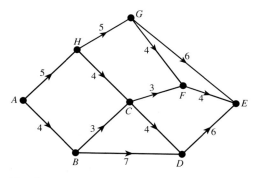

Use dynamic programming to minimise the longest time that the plane has to be airborne.

5 A maximin problem is solved by the route shown below.

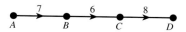

(a) What is the maximin value?

(b) What can be said about any route from A to D?

6 The diagram shows a network for which $a < b$ and $c < d$.

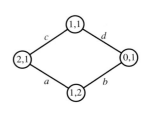

(a) Find an expression for the maximin.

(b) Find an expression for the minimax.

(c) Hence draw networks for which

    (i) the maximin is less than the minimax,

    (ii) the maximin is greater than the minimax.

7 The diagram shows a network with (stage, state) variables and costs.

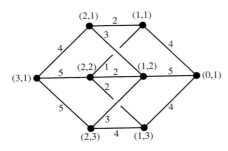

Set up and complete dynamic programming tabulations to find the

(a) maximin,

(b) minimax.

Miscellaneous exercise 4

1 The diagram shows a network with (stage, state) variables at the nodes and costs on the arcs.

Set up and complete a dynamic programming tabulation to find the route from (3, 1) to (0, 1) for which the minimum cost is a maximum (the maximin route).   (OCR, adapted)

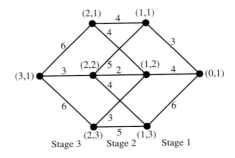

2 The diagram shows three stages in a manufacturing process. The nodes are labelled using (stage, state) and the values on the arcs represent profits in £.

Set up a dynamic programming tabulation, working backwards from stage 0, to find the route that gives the greatest profit.   (OCR, adapted)

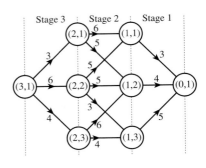

3 A factory needs a particular raw material for part of its production. There are three suppliers, A, B and C of the raw material but their charges vary according to the month. The raw material from the three suppliers varies slightly and this necessitates a changeover cost to the factory. This cost depends on the supplier of the raw material during the previous month. During March the factory is set up for supplier A and at the end of June it is to return to this state.

The changeover costs, in pounds, are as follows.

		To		
		A	B	C
	A	0	20	24
From	B	16	0	16
	C	20	16	0

The costs, in pounds, of the raw material from the suppliers for the three months are as follows.

		Month		
		April	May	June
	A	60	70	50
Supplier	B	40	60	80
	C	20	40	60

(a) Complete a network to illustrate the possible ways that the factory may purchase the raw material during the three months.

(b) Find the total cost incurred if the factory purchases the raw material from supplier B during April, supplier C during May and supplier A during June.

(c) Use dynamic programming to find the shortest path through the network that corresponds to the minimum cost to the factory. Describe the purchasing plan that the factory should adopt and state the minimum cost.   (AQA, adapted)

4 A student is comparing the use of different algorithms for solving shortest path problems. For a graph with n nodes, the student obtains the following formulae for the numbers of operations needed:

Dijkstra's algorithm $1.5n^2 - 2.5n + 1$,
Dynamic programming $2n^3 - 9n^2 + 14n - 7$.

(a) Hence comment on the relative merits of using Dijkstra's algorithm.

(b) What advantage does dynamic programming have?

5 The directed network below models different problems in this question.

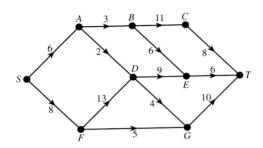

(a) (i) The network represents a set of routes, with the weights on the arcs representing distances in metres. Use dynamic programming to find the shortest route from S to T. (You must demonstrate your use of the algorithm.)

(ii) The network represents a set of pipes, with the weights representing pipe capacities in litres per second. Find the maximum flow which can pass from S to T and show how it is achieved. You are not required to use an algorithm to find this maximum flow, but you should prove that it is maximal.

(iii) The network is an activity network, with the weights representing activity durations in days. Use an appropriate algorithm to find the critical path and the shortest time for completion of the entire project.

(b) The network now represents routes along which a cargo plane can fly in moving from S to T. The weights on the arcs represent profits in £1000s which can be made by shifting cargoes from airport to airport en route. Explain which type of network from part (a) is most useful in trying to find the most profitable route, and give the largest profit.

(AQA, adapted)

6 A company is planning three building projects, A, B and C, to be completed at the rate of one per year. The costs of each project depend on which of the other projects have already been completed, as given in the table.

(a) Draw a network diagram to represent this information, using

stage = projects still to be completed.

(b) Find the building programs for which

(i) the total cost is least,

(ii) the greatest annual cost is minimal,

(iii) the least annual cost is maximal.

(c) Alter just the £9,500,000 cost in order to make the routes for (b)(ii), (ii) and (iii) different from each other.

Completed	Costs (£100,000s)		
	A	B	C
–	70	60	52
A	–	65	61
B	85	–	68
C	80	70	–
A, B	–	–	80
A, C	–	85	–
B, C	95	–	–

7 The network in the figure represents the direct
   routes between seven towns. The weights
   indicated on the arcs record the time, in
   minutes, taken to travel the route.

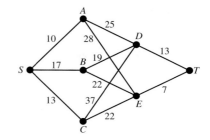

   (a) Use dynamic programming starting at T, to
       determine the minimum total time to travel
       between towns S and T. In your solution, carefully
       identify the stages, states, actions and values.

   (b) Identify the route with the minimum time.

   (c) State one advantage and one disadvantage of using dynamic programming in this
       context rather than an algorithm such as Dijkstra's.   (OCR, adapted)

8 Each Saturday a speciality cake baker takes orders for the week ahead. One week the orders
   are as shown in the table.

Day cakes are required	Monday	Tuesday	Wednesday	Thursday	Friday
Number of cakes	1	2	5	3	2

The baker can make up to four cakes on any one day, and can store up to and including
three cakes overnight. The cost of making each cake is £6, and the cost of storing a cake
overnight is £0.50 (to be charged before storage). Cakes can be stored for more than one
night. The daily overheads charge is £2.50 for each day that the baker is making cakes, but
there is no overheads charge if no cakes are made. At the start and end of the week there
must be no cakes in storage.

The baker wants to use dynamic programming to plan the production of the cakes so as to
minimise the total costs.

The days will be the stages, the number of cakes in storage at the start of each day will be
the states, and the number of cakes made each day will be the actions for this problem.

Set up a dynamic programming tabulation, working backwards from the end of the week,
with columns for the stages, states, actions, number of cakes to be stored at the end of the
day, daily costs and total costs. Use your tabulation to find the optimal production
strategy.   (OCR)

9 The figure shows a network labelled with (stage, state)
   variables, and with costs on the arcs.

   Complete a dynamic programming tabulation
   showing stages, states, actions, a column for
   recording the maximum cost on the route and
   a column for recording the minimax (the
   minimum of the maximum) costs.

   Find the route with the minimax total
   cost.   (OCR)

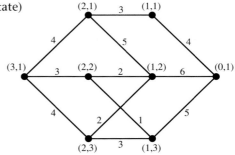

10 The figure shows a network with costs on the arcs.

Construct a dynamic programming tabulation showing stages, states, actions and a column for costs. Complete the table and find the route with the minimum total cost. (OCR, adapted)

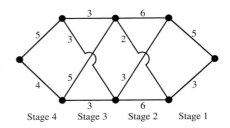

Stage 4   Stage 3   Stage 2   Stage 1

11 The Rolling Pebbles are choosing which venues to include on a short tour.

On Monday they will play at one of *A*, *B* and *C*; on Tuesday they will play at one of *D*, *E* and *F*; on Wednesday they will play at one of *G*, *H* and *I*; they return home on Thursday.

The figure shows the venues, labelled using (stage, state). The weights on the edges show the expected profit (in £10,000) from playing at each venue.

Use dynamic programming, working backwards from Thursday, to find which venues should be played on which day to maximise the total profit. (OCR, adapted)

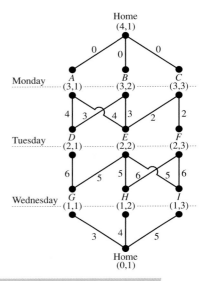

5 Game theory

This chapter looks at the analysis of situations where two competitors are both making decisions which affect each other. When you have completed it you should

- know what a two-person zero-sum game is
- be able to determine a play-safe strategy
- know what is meant by the value of a game with a stable solution
- be able to simplify games by using dominance arguments
- be able to find optimal mixed strategies for a game with no stable solution
- know how to convert a two-person zero-sum game into a linear programming problem.

5.1 Zero-sum games

In D1 and the previous chapters of this book, you have considered a variety of techniques of decision mathematics. As you have seen, most of these methods were developed to address business or military applications.

However, in business or military applications not only are you making decisions but so are your competitors or potential enemies. So far this important aspect of decision mathematics has been ignored and it is the purpose of this final chapter to remedy this omission.

The general idea of studying mathematically the consequences of decisions being made simultaneously by two or more competitors is called **game theory**. This theory has become a vital component of studies of competitive behaviour ranging from general interpersonal relationships to peace negotiations. In this chapter you will study the particular case of what is called a **two-person zero-sum game**.

The 'two-person' aspect has an obvious meaning: you will be considering cases where there are just two competitors. The 'zero-sum' aspect means that you will be studying cases where the gain for one party is exactly matched by the loss for the other. In zero-sum games you cannot achieve the ideal of a 'win-win' situation.

The idea of two-person zero-sum games can be illustrated by considering the game of 'stone-scissors-paper'. In this game, the two players simultaneously show either a fist representing stone, or two fingers representing scissors or an open palm representing paper.

The winner is determined by the following rules.

- Stone blunts and therefore beats scissors.
- Scissors cut and therefore beat paper.
- Paper wraps around and therefore beats stone.

If both players show the same object then the game is drawn.

The possible outcomes of one game can be represented by what are called **pay-off matrices**, shown in Fig. 5.1.

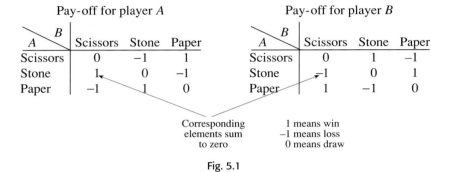

Pay-off for player A

A \ B	Scissors	Stone	Paper
Scissors	0	−1	1
Stone	1	0	−1
Paper	−1	1	0

Pay-off for player B

A \ B	Scissors	Stone	Paper
Scissors	0	1	−1
Stone	−1	0	1
Paper	1	−1	0

Corresponding
elements sum
to zero

1 means win
−1 means loss
0 means draw

Fig. 5.1

The 'zero-sum' nature of this game is demonstrated by the fact that each pair of corresponding elements has a sum of zero. Since one array of pay-offs is simply the negative of the other it is conventional to write a single pay-off matrix for a game, the one corresponding to the player (A in Fig. 5.1) whose choices are written on the left side of the matrix.

> A **two-person zero-sum game** is one between two players such that whatever one player gains the other loses.
>
> A **pay-off matrix** for such a game is a rectangular array of numbers representing the outcomes of each possible pair of decisions. The **outcomes** are the pay-offs to the player whose choices are on the left side of the matrix.

5.2 Play-safe strategies

Consider a game with pay-offs as shown in Fig. 5.2.

If player A chooses option 1 then A may lose as much as £1M. Whereas choosing option 2 guarantees that A will at least break even. In practice, many players would ignore the riskier option 1 and 'play safe' with option 2.

		Player B	
		1	2
Player A	1	£3M	−£1M
	2	£0	£1M

Fig. 5.2

> A **play-safe** strategy is to choose the option whose worst outcome is as good as possible.

When determining play-safe strategies, the working can be laid out as in the next two examples.

Example 5.2.1

Two players, *A* and *B*, play a game with the pay-off matrix shown.

(a) What is the outcome if both players play safe?

(b) Can either player improve their strategy if they know the other will play safe?

A \ B	1	2
1	3	−4
2	−3	1
3	2	−2

(a) Put an extra column to the right to show the worst outcome for *A* in each row. Thus, if *A* plays option 1, *A* may gain 3 or gain −4; the worst outcome is gaining −4, that is losing 4. Similarly the worst outcomes for options 2 and 3 are −3 and −2. Thus the best of the worst outcomes is −2, indicated by the arrow. This is *A*'s play-safe strategy.

A \ B	1	2	Worst outcome for A
1	3	−4	−4
2	−3	1	−3
3	2	−2	−2 ←
Worst outcome for B	3	1	

Similarly an extra row at the bottom shows *B*'s worst outcomes, which are losing 3 and 1. The best of these worst outcomes is 1, indicated by the arrow.

Thus, playing safe means *A* chooses option 3 and *B* chooses option 2. The outcome is that *A* loses 2 and *B* gains 2.

(b) If *B* plays safe, *A* can improve the pay-off to +1 by choosing option 2.

If *A* plays safe, *B* can do no better than choose option 2.

Example 5.2.2

For a game with the pay-off matrix in the figure, find the outcome if both players adopt play-safe strategies. Show that neither player can improve on this outcome by adopting a different strategy.

$$\begin{pmatrix} -1 & 0 & 1 \\ -2 & 1 & 3 \\ -3 & 0 & -4 \end{pmatrix}$$

The pay-off matrix is now given without explanatory notation about who is winning and who is losing. This will now be the convention in exercises and examples.

The table shows the play-safe strategies. So A chooses option 1 for a gain of at least -1 and B chooses option 1 for a gain of at least 1. A change of option for A would lose 2 or 3 and a change for B would break even or lose 1. It is in both players' interests to adopt the play-safe strategy.

A \\ B	1	2	3	Worst outcome for A
1	−1	0	1	−1 ←
2	−2	1	3	−2
3	−3	0	−4	−4
Worst outcome for B	−1 ↑	1	3	

From here on the extra row and column in the table will be labelled 'Row min(imum)' and 'Col(umn) max(imum)' instead of 'Worst outcome for A' and 'Worst outcome for B' respectively.

5.3   Stable solutions

The two examples of Section 5.2 illustrate that adopting a play-safe strategy may or may not be advantageous for a player.

If, as in Example 5.2.2, there is no incentive for either player to change from a play-safe strategy, then the game is said to have a **stable** solution.

Consider again the stable solution of Example 5.2.2, shown in Fig. 5.3.

You will have noticed that under this solution:

    A can guarantee to win at least
    max(row min) $= -1$;

    B can guarantee A will win at most
    min(column max) $= -1$.

The crucial result is that, for this matrix, the maximum of the row minima is equal to the minimum of the column maxima.

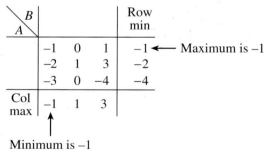

Fig. 5.3

A two-person zero-sum game has a **stable solution** if and only if

    max(row minima) = min(column maxima).

If a game has a stable solution, then both players should adopt a play-safe strategy and the pay-off from these strategies is called the **value** of the game.

Example 5.3.1
Determine whether the following games have stable solutions and, if so, state the value of the game.

(a) $\begin{pmatrix} 0 & -1 & 1 \\ 1 & 0 & -1 \\ -1 & 1 & 0 \end{pmatrix}$ (b) $\begin{pmatrix} -2 & 1 & 2 \\ 5 & 2 & 6 \\ 1 & -3 & 3 \end{pmatrix}$

(a) Each row minimum $= -1$, so max(row min) $= -1$.

Each column maximum $= +1$, so min(col max) $= 1$.

As max(row min) $\neq$ min(col max), there is no stable solution.

(b) The row minima are -2, 2 and -3, so max(row min) $= 2$.

The column maxima are 5, 2 and 6, so min(col max) $= 2$.

As max(row min) $\doteq$ min(col max), the game has a stable solution. The value of the game is the common value of max(row min) and min(col max), 2.

One idea which you can sometimes use to simplify the process of finding a solution to a problem is that of **dominance**.

Consider, for example, a game with the pay-off matrix in Fig. 5.4.

B should never choose options 1 and 4 because each element of column 1 and of column 4 is greater than or equal to the corresponding element of column 2. Thus the minimum of columns 1, 2 and 4 is always the element in column 2; column 2 is said to 'dominate' column 1 and column 4. Therefore you only need to consider the matrix in Fig. 5.5.

Similarly, in Fig. 5.5, each element of row 3 is less than the corresponding element of row 2, so A should never choose option 3. This leaves just the 2×2 matrix in Fig. 5.6 to be considered.

In fact, this has a stable solution when A chooses option 2 and B chooses option 3. The game therefore has value 1.

A \ B	1	2	3	4
1	5	-4	0	5
2	4	3	1	3
3	6	2	-2	3

Fig. 5.4

A \ B	2	3
1	-4	0
2	3	1
3	2	-2

Fig. 5.5

A \ B	2	3
1	-4	0
2	3	1

Fig. 5.6

A row of a pay-off matrix can be ignored if each element is less than or equal to the corresponding element of another row.

A column of a pay-off matrix can be ignored if each element is greater than or equal to the corresponding element of another column.

This process of ignoring rows or columns of a matrix is called **dominance**.

Exercise 5A

1 A two-person zero-sum game has pay-off matrix $\begin{pmatrix} 3 & -2 & 1 & -2 \\ 1 & -1 & 0 & 1 \\ -2 & 4 & 2 & -3 \end{pmatrix}$. Write down the matrix of pay-offs for the second player.

2 For the following games, determine the play-safe strategies for each player and the outcomes.

(a) $\begin{pmatrix} 5 & 4 \\ 6 & 3 \end{pmatrix}$ (b) $\begin{pmatrix} 1 & 2 \\ 4 & 3 \end{pmatrix}$ (c) $\begin{pmatrix} -4 & 0 & 2 & -2 \\ 3 & -5 & -2 & 0 \\ -3 & 1 & -5 & -2 \end{pmatrix}$ (d) $\begin{pmatrix} 4 & -3 \\ -4 & 3 \\ 0 & -4 \end{pmatrix}$

3 For each of the games in Question 2, determine if there is a stable solution. State the value of any game with a stable solution.

4 Determine if the following zero-sum games have stable solutions.

(a) $\begin{pmatrix} 4 & 5 \\ 7 & 6 \end{pmatrix}$ (b) $\begin{pmatrix} 5 & -4 \\ -5 & 4 \end{pmatrix}$ (c) $\begin{pmatrix} -4 & -3 & -2 & -1 \\ 3 & 2 & 1 & 0 \\ 2 & 1 & 0 & -1 \\ -5 & -4 & -3 & -2 \end{pmatrix}$ (d) $\begin{pmatrix} 0 & 2 \\ 4 & 6 \\ 8 & 10 \end{pmatrix}$

5 Determine play-safe strategies for the game $\begin{pmatrix} -3 & -6 & 2 & -12 \\ 12 & -11 & -5 & 7 \\ 4 & 7 & 3 & 6 \end{pmatrix}$. Can either player improve their pay-off by changing from this strategy assuming that the other still plays safe?

6 Two teams have to decide on their strategies for a cup final. Neither knows what the other will do. The probabilities of United winning with each combination of tactics is as shown in the figure.

		City		
		X	Y	Z
United	1	0.2	0.6	0.1
	2	0.3	0.5	0.6
	3	0.1	0.4	0.4

(a) Explain why United should never adopt strategy number 3.

(b) Which strategy should City never use?

(c) Reduce the table to a 2 × 2 pay-off matrix. Find the play-safe strategies for each team.

(d) Which strategy would you advise United to play? Explain your answer.

5.4   Mixed strategies

You can only be certain that a play-safe strategy is the best for a player when a game has a stable solution. Fortunately, there is a technique which allows you to find optimal strategies for all two-person zero-sum games. This technique uses the idea of a **mixed strategy** in which, rather than settle on a single option, a player has some likelihood of choosing any of the options. To illustrate the idea of this method, consider the game with the pay-off matrix shown in Fig. 5.7, and suppose that the game is played repeatedly.

A \ B	1	2
1	3	0
2	-1	2

Fig. 5.7

Suppose *A* adopts a mixed strategy of sometimes choosing option 1 and sometimes choosing option 2. Let *p* be the probability of choosing option 1; the probability of choosing option 2 is then $1 - p$.

If *B* chooses option 1

A gains 3 with probability *p* and gains −1 with probability $1 - p$. The expected pay-off is therefore

$$3p + (-1)(1 - p) = 3p - 1 + p = 4p - 1.$$

You can represent this graphically, as shown in Fig. 5.8.

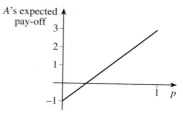

Fig. 5.8

If *B* chooses option 2

A gains 0 with probability *p* and gains 2 with probability $1 - p$. The expected pay-off is therefore

$$0p + 2(1 - p) = 2 - 2p.$$

You can represent this on the same diagram as Fig. 5.8, now shown as Fig. 5.9.

The two lines in Fig. 5.9 cross when $4p - 1 = 2 - 2p$, that is when $p = \frac{1}{2}$. For any value of *p*, *A* can expect a pay-off that is at least the value given by the solid line in Fig. 5.10.

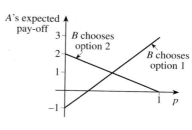

Fig. 5.9

If *A* chooses a value of *p* less than $\frac{1}{2}$, then *B*'s option 1 gives an expected pay-off less than 1, and *B*'s option 2 gives an expected pay-off greater than 1. For example, if $p = \frac{1}{3}$ the expected pay-off for *A* is $4 \times \frac{1}{3} - 1 = \frac{1}{3}$ if *B* chooses option 1. The expected pay-off is $2 - 2 \times \frac{1}{3} = \frac{4}{3}$ if *B* chooses option 2. So *A* can expect to receive at least $\frac{1}{3}$.

Similarly, if *A* chooses a value of *p* greater than $\frac{1}{2}$, then *B*'s option 2 gives a pay-off less than 1, but *B*'s option 1 gives a pay-off greater than 1.

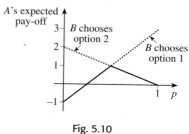

Fig. 5.10

However, if $p = \frac{1}{2}$ then the expected pay-off will be 1 whatever *B* chooses. *A* can therefore guarantee an expected pay-off of 1 by choosing each option with probability $\frac{1}{2}$. This is illustrated by the peak in the solid line in Fig. 5.10. This expected pay-off of 1 is the greatest that *A* can guarantee.

The method that you have just used to find the maximum expected pay-off should remind you of linear programming ideas.

The solid line in Fig. 5.11 can be considered to be part of the boundary of a convex feasible region.

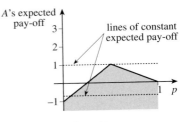

Fig. 5.11

Across this region you can slide a horizontal line. Feasible points on this line all represent the same expected pay-off. When this line touches the highest vertex, the maximum expected pay-off has been reached.

You can carry out a similar analysis for a mixed strategy adopted by B. Let B choose options 1 and 2 with probabilities q and $1 - q$ respectively. Then the expected pay-offs to B are

If A chooses option 1 B loses $3q + 0(1 - q) = 3q$;

If A chooses option 2 B loses $(-1)q + 2(1 - q) = -q + 2 - 2q = 2 - 3q$.

The values of $3q$ and $2 - 3q$ are equal when $3q = 2 - 3q$, that is $q = \frac{1}{3}$. For this value of q, the expected pay-off is then 1 whatever A does.

The following should now be clear. For the game $\begin{pmatrix} 3 & 0 \\ -1 & 2 \end{pmatrix}$,

- A should choose options 1 and 2 with probabilities $\frac{1}{2}$ and $\frac{1}{2}$ respectively,
- B should choose options 1 and 2 with probabilities $\frac{1}{3}$ and $\frac{2}{3}$ respectively.

If both play this way, then A can expect to gain 1 and B to lose 1. The value of the game is 1.

Example 5.4.1
Determine optimal strategies for the game with pay-off matrix $\begin{pmatrix} 6 & -2 \\ -3 & -1 \end{pmatrix}$, and draw a graph to illustrate this from A's point of view.

Let A choose options 1 and 2 with probabilities p and $1 - p$ respectively.

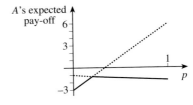

Then the expected pay-offs under B's two choices are $6p + (-3)(1 - p) = 9p - 3$ and $(-2)p + (-1)(1 - p) = -p - 1$.

These pay-offs are equal when $9p - 3 = -p - 1$, which gives $p = \frac{1}{5}$.

The expected pay-off is then $9 \times \frac{1}{5} - 3 = -1\frac{1}{5}$.

Now that you know the game's value of $-1\frac{1}{5}$, you can use it to determine B's strategy. Let B choose options 1 and 2 with probabilities q and $1 - q$ respectively.

Then the expected pay-off to B when A chooses option 1 is

$$-6q - (-2)(1 - q) = 2 - 8q = 1\frac{1}{5},$$

giving $q = \frac{1}{10}$.

A should choose option 1 with probability $\frac{1}{5}$ and B should choose option 1 with probability $\frac{1}{10}$.

Notice that you could also work out B's strategy from the alternative equation derived from A choosing option 2. Thus $(-3)q + (-1)(1-q) = -1\frac{1}{5}$. This also gives $q = \frac{1}{10}$.

In practice, both players should choose their options using a randomising device with the correct probabilities.

5.5   2 × *n* games

The graphical method of Section 5.4 was introduced with **2 × 2 games**, that is games with pay-off matrices which have 2 rows and 2 columns. The method can be extended to 2 × *n* games, that is games with pay-off matrices which have 2 rows and *n* columns.

Consider, for example, the game with the pay-off matrix shown in Fig. 5.12.

Let A choose options 1 and 2 with probabilities p and $1 - p$, respectively. Then the expected pay-offs under B's choices can be represented by the straight line graphs in Fig. 5.13.

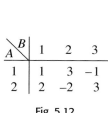

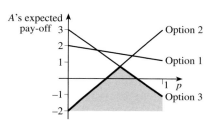

Fig. 5.12   Fig. 5.13

Whatever B's strategy, A can guarantee expected pay-offs in the shaded region bounded by the thick line in Fig. 5.13.

From Fig. 5.13, A should therefore choose option 1 with probability p, determined by the point of intersection of the lines corresponding to B's option 2 and option 3.

This point of intersection is given by

$$3p + (-2)(1-p) = (-1)p + 3(1-p), \quad \text{which gives} \quad p = \tfrac{5}{9}.$$

The game thus has a value V given by

$$V = 3 \times \tfrac{5}{9} + (-2) \times \left(1 - \tfrac{5}{9}\right) = \tfrac{15}{9} - \tfrac{8}{9} = \tfrac{7}{9}.$$

B should ignore option 1 and choose option 2 with probability q, where

$$3q + (-1)(1-q) = \tfrac{7}{9}, \quad \text{or} \quad (-2)q + 3(1-q) = \tfrac{7}{9}.$$

Either way, $q = \tfrac{4}{9}$.

A general procedure for solving any 2 × *n* game between the first player A and the second player B which does not have a stable solution is as follows.

To solve a $2 \times n$ game between A and B,

Step 1   Assign probabilities p and $1 - p$ to the two options for A.

Step 2   Plot A's expected pay-off under each of B's options as lines on a graph of pay-off against p.

Step 3   Shade the region which lies underneath *every* line.

Step 4   Find the value of p at the highest point of the shaded region by solving simultaneous equations.

Step 5   Use this value of p to find the value, V, of the game.

Step 6   Assign probability q to one of those options for B which determine the highest point of the shaded region.

Step 7   Find the value of q which gives B an expected pay-off of $-V$, under either of A's options.

Example 5.5.1

Determine the optimal mixed strategies and the value for the game with the given pay-off matrix.

A \ B	1	2	3	4
1	1	2.5	2	5
2	7	−0.5	8	−3
3	6	−1	4	−5

Row 3 is dominated by row 2 and so can be ignored. Column 3 is now dominated by column 1 and can also be ignored. The matrix is thus reduced to $2 \times n$ and the method given in the shaded box is appropriate. The new matrix is shown on the right.

A \ B	1	2	4
1	1	2.5	5
2	7	−0.5	−3

Step 1   Let A choose option 1 with probability p.

Step 2   If B plays option 1, A gains $p + 7(1 - p) = 7 - 6p$.

If B plays option 2, A gains $2.5p + (-0.5)(1 - p) = 3p - 0.5$.

If B plays option 4, A gains $5p + (-3)(1 - p) = 8p - 3$.

You can then plot these pay-off functions.

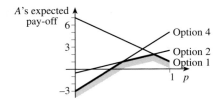

Step 3   Shade the region that lies under every pay-off line.

Note that, as in linear programming problems, it is easier not to shade the whole area, but simply to outline the area by shading.

Step 4 The highest point of the shaded region is where the pay-off lines for options 1 and 2 intersect, which is where

$$7 - 6p = 3p - 0.5, \quad \text{that is where} \quad p = \tfrac{5}{6}.$$

Step 5 Let V be the value of the game.

Then $\quad V = 1 \times \tfrac{5}{6} + 7\left(1 - \tfrac{5}{6}\right) = \tfrac{5}{6} + \tfrac{7}{6} = 2.$

Step 6 The two pay-off lines which give the value of p are those for options 1 and 2. Let q be the probability that B plays option 1, so $1 - q$ is the probability that B plays option 2.

Step 7 Then $1q + 2.5(1 - q) = 2$, giving $\quad q = \tfrac{1}{3}.$

The game has value 2. A should choose options 1 and 2 with probabilities $\tfrac{5}{6}$ and $\tfrac{1}{6}$ respectively. B should choose options 1 and 2 with probabilities $\tfrac{1}{3}$ and $\tfrac{2}{3}$ respectively.

An $n \times 2$ game can be transformed into a $2 \times n$ game by interchanging the two players. In order that the pay-offs continue to relate to the player whose choices are listed at the left, the signs of all the entries in the matrix should be changed.

Example 5.5.2

Find the value of the game with the pay-off matrix $\begin{pmatrix} -2 & 0 \\ 1 & -2 \\ -3 & 2 \end{pmatrix}.$

Consider instead the game with matrix $\begin{pmatrix} 2 & -1 & 3 \\ 0 & 2 & -2 \end{pmatrix}$, where the rows and columns have been interchanged, and the signs of the entries have been changed.

Let A choose option 1 with probability p.

If B plays option 1, A gains $2p + 0(1 - p) = 2p.$

If B plays option 2, A gains

$$(-1)p + 2(1 - p) = 2 - 3p.$$

If B plays option 3, A gains

$$3p + (-2)(1 - p) = 5p - 2.$$

You can find the value of p by solving the equation arising from equating the pay-offs of options 2 and 3.

Thus $2 - 3p = 5p - 2$, giving $\quad p = \tfrac{1}{2}.$

The value $V = (-1) \times \tfrac{1}{2} + 2\left(1 - \tfrac{1}{2}\right) = \tfrac{1}{2}.$

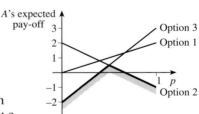

Recalling that the signs of the original game were changed, the value of the original game is therefore $-\tfrac{1}{2}.$

Exercise 5B

1 A two-person zero-sum game has the pay-off matrix
   shown in the figure.

   Suppose that Ann uses random numbers to choose
   strategy M with probability p.

		Ben		
		X	Y	Z
Ann	M	3	−2	1
	N	1	3	2

   (a) Find the expected gains when Ben chooses each
       of strategies X, Y and Z.

   (b) Use a graphical method to find the optimum value for p.

   (c) State the expected value of the game for both Ann and Ben.

   (d) Which strategy should Ben never use?

2 A two-person game has pay-off matrix shown in the figure.

   (a) Suppose that the first player chooses strategy A with
       probability p. Find the expected gains for the first
       player when the second player chooses each of
       strategies X and Y.

	X	Y
A	5	2
B	3	4

   (b) Suppose that the second player chooses strategy X with probability q. Find the expected
       gains for the first player when the first player chooses each of strategies A and B.

   (c) Find the value of the game and the corresponding values of p and q.

3 Find the values of the following games.

   (a) $\begin{pmatrix} 4 & 1 \\ 3 & 5 \end{pmatrix}$

   (b) $\begin{pmatrix} 2 & 1 \\ 1 & 3 \end{pmatrix}$

   (c) $\begin{pmatrix} -1 & 3 \\ 2 & -1 \end{pmatrix}$

4 (a) Use dominance to reduce the game with pay-off matrix $\begin{pmatrix} 6 & 7 & 2 \\ 1 & 3 & 5 \end{pmatrix}$ to a 2 × 2 game.

   (b) Hence find the value of this game.

5 The Rolling Pebbles have been playing as a band for many years. When they tour they
   sometimes play old songs, they sometimes play new songs and they sometimes play a
   mixture of old and new songs. The table shows the audience reaction (as a score out of 10)
   for each of the possible combinations. High scores are good.

		Audience		
		Young	Mixed	Older
	Old	1	3	8
Songs played	Mixture	3	1	2
	New	8	5	3

Explain why, according to these data, the band should never choose to play a mixture of old and new songs.

The band do not know whether their audience will be young, older or of mixed ages. Suppose that they choose to play old songs with probability p and new songs with probability $1 - p$.

(a) Calculate, in terms of p, the expected reaction from each of the three types of audience.

(b) Use a graphical method to decide what value p should take to maximise the minimum expected reaction from part (a). Mark clearly on your graph the vertex where the optimal value occurs.   (OCR)

5.6 $m \times n$ games

The graphical method of Section 5.5 cannot be applied when the pay-off matrix has more than 2 rows. Fortunately, however, it is possible to convert the ideas of Section 5.5 into linear programming form. This method will be illustrated with a 3×2 game but can be applied to a game of any size.

Consider the game with pay-off matrix $\begin{pmatrix} 2 & 4 \\ 5 & 2 \\ 1 & 6 \end{pmatrix}$.

Suppose the first player, A, chooses options 1, 2 and 3 with probabilities p_1, p_2 and p_3 respectively. Then the expected pay-offs are $2p_1 + 5p_2 + 1p_3$ and $4p_1 + 2p_2 + 6p_3$, depending upon which strategy the second player chooses. Let v be the pay-off which the first player is trying to maximise. Then, in linear programming format, the problem is

maximise v,

subject to $v \leqslant 2p_1 + 5p_2 + 1p_3,$ These two conditions ensure that
$v \leqslant 4p_1 + 2p_2 + 6p_3,$ v is the smaller of $2p_1 + 5p_2 + 1p_3$
$p_1 + p_2 + p_3 \leqslant 1,$ and $4p_1 + 2p_2 + 6p_3.$
$p_1, p_2, p_3 \geqslant 0.$

Note the use of the condition $p_1 + p_2 + p_3 \leqslant 1$. Because all the elements in the pay-off matrix are positive, v is bound to be positive. When v is maximised, $p_1 + p_2 + p_3$ will therefore automatically equal 1, as required, because they are all probabilities.

The problem can now be solved in the standard manner, using the Simplex method given in D1 Chapter 8. In D1, equation numbers will be written in circles; here they will be written in bold type. The tableau for the problem is over the page.

P	v	p_1	p_2	p_3	r	s	t		Equation
1	-1	0	0	0	0	0	0	0	**1**
0	0	1	1	1	1	0	0	1	**2**
0	1	-2	-5	-1	0	1	0	0	**3**
0	1	-4	-2	-6	0	0	1	0	**4**
1	0	-4	-2	-6	0	0	1	0	$\mathbf{5 = 1 + 8}$
0	0	1	1	1	1	0	0	1	$\mathbf{6 = 2}$
0	0	2	-3	5	0	1	-1	0	$\mathbf{7 = 3 - 8}$
0	1	-4	-2	-6	0	0	1	0	$\mathbf{8 = 4}$
1	0	0	-8	4	0	2	-1	0	$\mathbf{9 = 5 + 4 \times 11}$
0	0	0	$\frac{5}{2}$	$-\frac{3}{2}$	1	$-\frac{1}{2}$	$\frac{1}{2}$	1	$\mathbf{10 = 6 - 11}$
0	0	1	$-\frac{3}{2}$	$\frac{5}{2}$	0	$\frac{1}{2}$	$-\frac{1}{2}$	0	$\mathbf{11 = \frac{1}{2} \times 7}$
0	1	0	-8	4	0	2	-1	0	$\mathbf{12 = 8 + 4 \times 11}$
1	0	0	0	$-\frac{4}{5}$	$\frac{16}{5}$	$\frac{2}{5}$	$\frac{3}{5}$	$\frac{16}{5}$	$\mathbf{13 = 9 + 8 \times 14}$
0	0	0	1	$-\frac{3}{5}$	$\frac{2}{5}$	$-\frac{1}{5}$	$\frac{1}{5}$	$\frac{2}{5}$	$\mathbf{14 = \frac{2}{5} \times 10}$
0	0	1	0	$\frac{8}{5}$	$\frac{3}{5}$	$\frac{1}{5}$	$-\frac{1}{5}$	$\frac{3}{5}$	$\mathbf{15 = 11 + \frac{3}{2} \times 14}$
0	1	0	0	$-\frac{4}{5}$	$\frac{16}{5}$	$\frac{2}{5}$	$\frac{3}{5}$	$\frac{16}{5}$	$\mathbf{16 = 12 + 8 \times 14}$
1	0	$\frac{1}{2}$	0	0	$\frac{7}{2}$	$\frac{1}{2}$	$\frac{1}{2}$	$\frac{7}{2}$	$\mathbf{17 = 13 + \frac{4}{5} \times 19}$
0	0	$\frac{3}{8}$	1	0	$\frac{5}{8}$	$-\frac{1}{8}$	$\frac{1}{8}$	$\frac{5}{8}$	$\mathbf{18 = 14 + \frac{3}{5} \times 19}$
0	0	$\frac{5}{8}$	0	1	$\frac{3}{8}$	$\frac{1}{8}$	$-\frac{1}{8}$	$\frac{3}{8}$	$\mathbf{19 = \frac{5}{8} \times 15}$
0	1	$\frac{1}{2}$	0	0	$\frac{7}{2}$	$\frac{1}{2}$	$\frac{1}{2}$	$\frac{7}{2}$	$\mathbf{20 = 16 + \frac{4}{5} \times 19}$

The game has value $\frac{7}{2}$. The first player should choose $p_1 = 0$, $p_2 = \frac{5}{8}$, $p_3 = \frac{3}{8}$.

The method just employed requires the elements of the pay-off matrix to be positive (to ensure that the sum of the probabilities equals 1). If this is not the case, then you can simply add the same number to every element, remembering that you have then increased the value by this number.

You will have seen that, although linear programming using the Simplex method allows you to solve problems of any size, in practice the working is very time consuming. For that reason, most of the problems you will consider in this section will be of a relatively small size.

Example 5.6.1

Convert the problem of Example 5.4.1, with pay-off matrix $\begin{pmatrix} 6 & -2 \\ -3 & -1 \end{pmatrix}$ into a linear programming problem. Find the optimum strategy for the first player by using the Simplex algorithm.

First, add 4 to every element, so that the pay-off matrix is now $\begin{pmatrix} 10 & 2 \\ 1 & 3 \end{pmatrix}$.

The problem is

$$\begin{aligned} \text{maximise} \quad & v - 4, \\ \text{subject to} \quad & v \leq 10p_1 + p_2, \\ & v \leq 2p_1 + 3p_2, \\ & p_1 + p_2 \leq 1, \\ & p_1, p_2 \geq 0. \end{aligned}$$

P	v	p_1	p_2	r	s	t		Equation
1	−1	0	0	0	0	0	−4	**1**
0	1	−10	−1	1	0	0	0	**2**
0	1	−2	−3	0	1	0	0	**3**
0	0	1	1	0	0	1	1	**4**
1	0	−2	−3	0	1	0	−4	**5 = 1 + 7**
0	0	−8	**2**	1	−1	0	0	**6 = 2 − 7**
0	1	−2	−3	0	1	0	0	**7 = 3**
0	0	1	1	0	0	1	1	**8 = 4**
1	0	−14	0	$\frac{3}{2}$	$-\frac{1}{2}$	0	−4	**9 = 5 + 3 × 10**
0	0	−4	1	$\frac{1}{2}$	$-\frac{1}{2}$	0	0	**10 = $\frac{1}{2}$ × 6**
0	1	−14	0	$\frac{3}{2}$	$-\frac{1}{2}$	0	0	**11 = 7 + 3 × 10**
0	0	**5**	0	$-\frac{1}{2}$	$\frac{1}{2}$	1	1	**12 = 8 − 10**
1	0	0	0	$\frac{1}{10}$	$\frac{9}{10}$	$\frac{14}{5}$	$-\frac{6}{5}$	**13 = 9 + 14 × 16**
0	0	0	1	$\frac{1}{10}$	$-\frac{1}{10}$	$\frac{4}{5}$	$\frac{4}{5}$	**14 = 10 + 4 × 16**
0	1	0	0	$\frac{1}{10}$	$\frac{9}{10}$	$\frac{14}{5}$	$\frac{14}{5}$	**15 = 11 + 14 × 16**
0	0	1	0	$-\frac{1}{10}$	$\frac{1}{10}$	$\frac{1}{5}$	$\frac{1}{5}$	**16 = $\frac{1}{5}$ × 12**

The game has value $-\frac{6}{5}$. The first player should play options 1 and 2 with probabilities $\frac{1}{5}$ and $\frac{4}{5}$, respectively.

Note that the second player's strategy can be found by a similar procedure or, more simply, by solving $6q - 2(1 - q) = -\frac{6}{5}$, giving $q = \frac{1}{10}$.

Exercise 5C

1 A two-person zero-sum game has pay-off matrix $\begin{pmatrix} 4 & 1 \\ 3 & 5 \end{pmatrix}$.

Suppose the first player chooses options 1 and 2 with probabilities p and q respectively. Let v be the expected pay-off.

Formulate this as a linear programming problem and hence find v.

2 A two-person zero-sum game has pay-off matrix $\begin{pmatrix} -1 & 3 \\ 2 & -1 \end{pmatrix}$. By first adding 2 to every

element, convert the game into a linear programming problem and hence find the value of the game.

3 For the game with pay-off matrix $\begin{pmatrix} 3 & 2 & 5 \\ 4 & 5 & 2 \\ 2 & 4 & 4 \end{pmatrix}$, suppose the first player chooses options 1, 2

and 3 with probabilities p, q and r respectively. Formulate, but do not solve, the problem of finding the game's value v as a linear programming problem.

Miscellaneous exercise 5

1 A game has pay-off matrix shown in the figure.

Show that this game has a stable solution and find the play-safe strategies for each player.

A \ B	1	2	3	4
1	6	−3	15	−11
2	7	1	9	5
3	−3	0	−5	8

2 The game 'stone-scissors-paper' has pay-off matrix shown.

(a) Suppose that the first player chooses stone, scissors and paper with probabilities p, q and $1 - p - q$ respectively. Find the expected gains when the second player chooses each of the strategies stone, scissors and paper.

(b) How can the first player guarantee an expected return of 0?

(c) What is the value of the game? Justify your answer.

	St	Sc	P
St	0	1	−1
Sc	−1	0	1
P	1	−1	0

3 The pay-off matrix for a zero-sum game between two players A and B is $A \begin{pmatrix} 3 & -2 \\ -2 & 1 \end{pmatrix}$.

(a) Show that the game does not have a stable solution.

Player A uses the mixed strategy defined by $(0.6, 0.4)$.

(b) Determine the expected pay-off for A if player B:

(i) plays column one;

(ii) plays column two;

(iii) adopts the strategy $(0.5, 0.5)$.

(c) Determine the optimal strategy for A and its expected pay-off.   (OCR)

4 Roland and Colleen play a two-person zero-sum game. The table shows the pay-off matrix for the game. The values in the table are the amounts won by Roland.

| | | Colleen | |
		Stick	Twist
Roland	Stick	−1	4
	Twist	3	−2

(a) Find Roland's and Colleen's play-safe strategies, and hence show that this game does not have a stable solution.

(b) (i) State which strategy Roland should choose if he knows that Colleen will choose her play-safe strategy.

(ii) State which strategy Colleen should choose if she knows that Roland will choose his play-safe strategy.

Roland and Colleen play the game a large number of times. Colleen uses random numbers to choose the Stick strategy with probability p.

(c) Show that the expected gain for Roland when he chooses the Stick strategy is given by $4 - 5p$, and find a similar expression for the expected gain for Roland when he chooses the Twist strategy.

(d) Use a graphical method to find the optimum value of p. (OCR)

5 Robin is playing a computer game in which he has to protect the environment. He chooses an energy source and the computer chooses the weather conditions.

The numbers of points scored by Robin under each of the combinations of energy type and weather conditions are shown in the table.

| | | Computer | | |
		Warm	Wet	Windy
	Atomic energy	−6	3	5
Robin	Bio-gas	2	4	6
	Coal	5	1	3

Robin is trying to maximise his points total and the computer tries to stop him.

(a) Explain why Robin should not choose Atomic energy and why the computer should not choose Windy weather.

(b) Find the play-safe strategies for the reduced game for Robin and for the computer, and hence show that this game does not have a stable solution.

Suppose that Robin uses random numbers to choose Bio-gas with probability p and Coal with probability $1 - p$.

(c) Show that the expected loss for the computer when it chooses Warm weather is given by $5 - 3p$, and find an expression for the expected loss when it chooses Wet weather.

(d) Use a graphical method to find the optimum value of p and the corresponding expected gain for Robin. (OCR)

6   Roy and Callum play a two-person zero-sum game. The table shows the pay-off matrix for the game. The values in the table are the amounts won by Roy.

		Callum	
		Strategy A	Strategy B
Roy	Strategy P	-1	1
	Strategy Q	4	-3

(a) Find Roy's and Callum's play-safe strategies, and show that this game does not have a stable solution.

(b) (i) State which strategy Roy should choose if he knows that Callum will always choose his play-safe strategy.

(ii) State which strategy Callum should choose if he knows that Roy will always choose his play-safe strategy.

Suppose that Roy uses random numbers to choose strategy P with probability p.

(c) Show that the expected gain for Callum when he chooses strategy A is given by $5p - 4$, and find a similar expression for the expected gain for Callum when he chooses strategy B.

(d) Use a graphical method to find the optimum value of p and the corresponding expected gain for Roy.

(OCR)

7   Rowena and Colin play a two-person zero-sum simultaneous-play game. The table shows the pay-off matrix for the game.

		Colin		
		Strategy X	Strategy Y	Strategy Z
Rowena	Strategy A	4	-1	2
	Strategy B	4	6	3
	Strategy C	1	2	-2

(a) Find Rowena's and Colin's play-safe strategies, and hence show that this game has a stable solution.

(b) Explain what having a stable solution means to the way the game is played.

(c) Explain why Colin will never choose strategy X, and hence reduce the game to give a 2×2 pay-off matrix.

Suppose that Colin uses random numbers to choose strategy Y with probability p.

(d) Show that the expected gain when Rowena chooses strategy A is given by $2 - 3p$ and find a similar expression for the expected gain when Rowena chooses her other strategy.

(e) Use a graphical method to find the optimum value of p and the corresponding expected gain for Colin.

(OCR)

8 Richard and Carol play a two-person zero-sum simultaneous-play game. The table shows the pay-off matrix for the game.

		Carol		
		Strategy X	Strategy Y	Strategy Z
Richard	Strategy A	2	3	-2
	Strategy B	-4	-1	-1
	Strategy C	-5	0	1

(a) Explain the meaning of the term zero-sum game.

(b) Find the play-safe strategies for both Richard and Carol, and hence show that this game does not have a stable solution.

(c) Suppose that Richard knows that Carol will use her play-safe strategy. Explain whether or not he should change from his play-safe strategy as found in part (b).

(d) Suppose that Carol knows that Richard will use his play-safe strategy. Explain whether or not she should change from her play-safe strategy as found in part (b).   (OCR)

9 Rose is playing a computer game in which she has to defend a planet from aliens. She chooses a defence strategy and the computer chooses an attack strategy.

The number of points scored by Rose with each combination of strategies is shown in the table.

		Computer		
		Fight	Shoot	Track
Rose	Delay	-2	-5	1
	Hide	3	4	6
	Negotiate	5	-1	2

Rose is trying to maximise the number of points that she scores, and the computer is trying to minimise the number of points that Rose scores.

(a) Find the play-safe strategy for Rose and for the computer, and hence show that this game does not have a stable solution.

(b) Explain why Rose will not choose the Delay strategy.

(c) Which strategy will the computer never choose to play?

Suppose that Rose uses random numbers to choose between her two remaining strategies, choosing the Hide strategy with probability p and the Negotiate strategy with probability $1 - p$.

(d) Find expressions for the expected gain for Rose when the computer chooses each of its remaining strategies.

(e) Calculate the value of p for Rose to maximise her guaranteed return.   (OCR)

10 Richard is playing a computer battle game in which he chooses a warrior and the computer chooses an opponent. Neither Richard nor the computer knows what the other has chosen.

The probabilities of Richard winning the battle with each combination of warrior and opponent are shown in the table. If Richard does not win, the computer wins. Both Richard and the computer are playing to win.

		Computer		
		Dragon	Elf	Fighter
	Argent	0.4	0.7	0.3
Richard	Bronze	0.5	0.6	0.8
	Crystal	0.2	0.5	0.1

(a) Explain why the computer should never choose Elf.

(b) Which warrior should Richard never choose?

(c) Use the information from parts (a) and (b) to reduce the table to a 2 × 2 matrix. Find the play-safe strategies for the reduced game for Richard and for the computer.

(d) Richard plays the game many times. What strategy should he use? Explain your answer.   (OCR)

Revision exercise

1 The adjacency matrix shown represents an incomplete matching.

(a) Draw a bipartite graph to represent the possible pairings and to show the incomplete matching.

(b) Use the Matching Augmentation algorithm to obtain a complete matching. Explain your method carefully.

$$\begin{array}{c c c c c}
 & E & F & G & H \\
A & 1 & 0 & 1 & 0 \\
B & 0 & 1 & 1 & 0 \\
C & 1 & 0 & 1 & 1 \\
D & 1 & 1 & 1 & 0
\end{array}$$

2 As part of their Leisure and Tourism course, some students are planning to produce a video to promote the attractions of their town. Some of the activities involved are listed below.

	Activity	Expected duration (days)	Preceded by
A	Visit possible locations	1	–
B	Plan storyboard and write script	2	–
C	Plan shooting schedule	1	A, B
D	Get permission at locations	1	C
E	Organise lighting, sound and equipment	2	C
F	Organise performers	1	C
G	Outdoor filming	2	D, E, F
H	Indoor filming	3	E, F
I	Editing and sound dubbing	1	G, H

(a) Copy and complete the activity schedule below, showing the earliest and latest start and finish times of each activity (assuming completion in the minimum possible time), and the float for each activity.

Activity	Earliest start	Latest start	Earliest finish	Latest finish	Float
A	0	1	1	2	1
B	0	0	2	2	0
C					
D					
E					
F	3	4	4	5	1
G					
H					
I					

(b) Find the minimum time for completion of the project.

(c) List the critical activities.

(d) Suppose that poor weather holds up the outdoor filming (activity G) by 1 day. Describe the effect that this will have on the total time to complete the project. (OCR)

3 The Rolling Pebbles have been invited to appear on three different talk shows. The shows are all at the same time, but in different places. The four members of the band have decided that one of them will not appear on any show, and that each of the other three will appear on a different show.

The scores in the table show how popular each band member is likely to be on each show. A higher score means that the band member is more popular. The band wants to find the allocation that gives the maximum total score.

| | | Band member | | | |
		Wart	Xenon	Yogi	Ziggy
	Local radio	5	6	3	4
Show	Midday TV	3	7	4	2
	National radio	7	8	6	4

(a) Explain how the figures in the table can be changed so that the problem becomes one of finding an allocation that gives a minimum non-negative total.

(b) Explain how to convert the adapted scores from part (a) into a square matrix on which the Hungarian algorithm can be used.

(c) Use the Hungarian algorithm, reducing rows first, to allocate the band members to the shows in the most appropriate way.   (OCR)

4 The diagram on the left shows an undirected network. S is the source and T is the sink. The values show the capacities of the arcs.

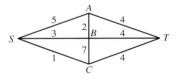 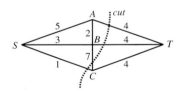

(a) Redraw the left diagram as a directed flow network.

A *cut* can be drawn through the undirected network, as shown in the diagram on the right.

(b) Define what is meant by a cut.

A cut can be described by listing the nodes which are on the source side, X, and the nodes which are on the sink side, Y. The cut shown has $X = \{S, A, B\}$ and $Y = \{C, T\}$.

(c) Write down the number of different cuts that are possible for this network (including the cut shown).

(d) List all the cuts from part (c), by giving the nodes in X and the nodes in Y, and calculate the value of each cut.

(e) Explaining your reasoning carefully, describe what you can conclude from the results of part (d).

5 Visitors to a stately home tour the house on one of a
   number of routes. The diagram shows these routes
   and the maximum flows in people per hour.

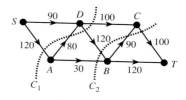

(a) List the eight possible routes from S to T.

(b) Calculate the values of the cuts C_1 and C_2, and
     explain what this tells you about the maximum
     flow from S to T.

(c) Find the maximum flow from S to T.

6 The activities involved in preparing a major archaeological dig are listed in the table
   below.

	Activity	Expected duration (days)	Number of people needed	Preceded by
A	Survey site	2	3	–
B	Aerial photography	2	2	A
C	Geophysics	5	2	A
D	Remove topsoil	2	3	A
E	Check records of previous digs	1	2	A
F	Dig investigation trench	4	5	D, E
G	Check old maps and public records	5	2	E
H	Computer analysis	3	2	B, C
I	Begin main excavation	10	5	F, G
J	Record findings	4	4	H, I

(a) Draw up a table showing the earliest and latest possible start and finish times for each
     activity (in days from the beginning of the project).

(b) Write down the critical activities.

The table below shows the number of people needed each day when using the earliest
starting date schedule. This schedule requires a minimum of nine people in the team.

Day number	1	2	3	4	5	6	7	8	9	10	11
Team size	3	3	9	9	9	9	9	9	7	7	5

Day number	12	13	14	15	16	17	18	19	20	21	22
Team size	5	5	5	5	5	5	5	4	4	4	4

(c) Draw up a schedule that is consistent with the earliest finish time but only needs seven
     people in the team.

                                                                          (OCR)

7   A relay team consists of four runners, *A, B, C* and *D*, each of whom runs one leg of the race. The best training times, in seconds, for each of the runners over each of the legs are given in the table.

	1st leg	2nd leg	3rd leg	4th leg
A	47	45	45	43
B	48	44	45	44
C	46	45	44	43
D	50	47	46	44

Use the Hungarian algorithm to decide which runner should be allocated to which leg of the race.

8   Jim is playing a space adventure game. He has found the alien headquarters and now has four turns to escape from the planet, or else perish. On each turn, Jim must play one of three tactics. He can attack, run away or dodge the aliens. The number of energy pods used up during the turn is shown in the first table.

Tactic	Energy pods used
Attack	2
Run away	1
Dodge	0

The number of squares that Jim travels with each of these tactics is shown in the second table.

	Energy pods remaining at start of turn				
	5	4	3	2	1
Attack	6	7	6	4	–
Run away	5	4	4	3	1
Dodge	1	2	1	1	0

Jim currently has five energy pods, and needs to maximise the number of squares that he travels in the four turns that he has left. He should finish the game with no energy pods remaining, but he needs at least one energy pod at the start of each of his four turns.

(a) Draw a network showing the action (*A, R* or *D*) and the cost (number of squares travelled) for each possible transaction.

(b) Set up a dynamic programming tabulation, with *stage* = 5 − *turn* (starting at Turn 4 and ending at Turn 1), *state* = *number of energy pods remaining*, and using action and cost as in part (a). Use your dynamic programming tabulation to find Jim's best strategy, and the number of squares that Jim travels using this strategy.   (OCR, adapted)

9 The diagram shows a network with (stage, state) variables at the nodes and costs on the arcs.

Use dynamic programming tabulations to find the routes from (3,1) to (0,1) for which the costs are

(a) minimum,   (b) maximum.

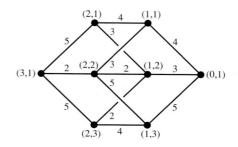

10 Rachael is playing a two-person zero-sum simultaneous-play game against her computer. The pay-off matrix is as shown.

	Computer		
	2	3	−2
Rachael	−4	−1	−1
	−5	0	1

Rachael decides to choose her options with probabilities p_1, p_2 and p_3 respectively, and wants to maximise the pay-off.

(a) By first adding 6 to every element in the pay-off matrix, formulate this as a linear programming problem.

(b) Show (but do not solve) the initial Simplex tableau.

11 An advertising campaign manager has a choice of three adverts (an old advert, the current advert or a new advert) and may select from three options:

      A: Change back to the old advert;

      B: Continue with the current advert;

      C: Run the new advert.

The possible choices and expected profits (in £1000s) are shown in the network below, together with (stage, state) labels.

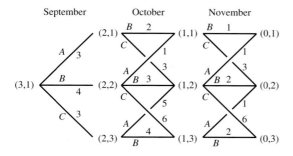

The manager wants to maximise the total profit.

Use a tabular approach to solve this dynamic programming problem, starting with Stage 0. State the maximum profit and the choices made to achieve it.   (OCR)

12 Minnie, Max and their friend Dominic have formed a quiz team. Much to their surprise they have reached the final of a mathematics quiz. They are required to nominate one team member to take part in a solo round.

The solo round will consist of 10 questions on one of three specialist subjects: Arabic, Babylonian or Chinese mathematics. The contestants do not know which of the specialist subjects has been chosen.

Based on their performances in rehearsal, the members of the team expect their scores out of 10 to be as given in the table below.

		Specialist subject		
		Arabic	Babylonian	Chinese
	Minnie	4	7	4
Solo player	Max	6	5	7
	Dominic	3	6	3

(a) Explain why Dominic should not be chosen to play the solo round.

(b) Dominic suggests tossing a coin and letting Minnie play the solo round if the coin comes up heads, and Max play if it comes up tails. Assuming that the coin is fair, calculate the expected score for each of the three possible specialist subjects.

(c) If, instead of using equal probabilities, they choose Minnie with probability p and Max with probability $1 - p$ find the expected score for each of the three possible specialist subjects.

(d) Minnie objects that this is not a repeated play situation and suggests that the team should use their play-safe strategy. Showing your working, find out which member of the team should play the solo round if they use this strategy.   (OCR)

Practice examination 1

Time 1 hour 20 minutes

Answer all the questions.

You are permitted to use a graphic calculator in this paper.

1 Five pupils receive the following votes for four positions of responsibility.

	A	B	C	D	E
Head prefect	5	7	7	5	6
Captain of sports	6	7	8	4	7
Library prefect	7	5	6	5	7
Charities prefect	6	5	7	6	7

It is intended to allocate the positions so as to maximise the total score.

(i) The Hungarian algorithm finds the allocation with the minimum total cost. State how this problem can be converted into a minimisation problem. [1]

(ii) The Hungarian algorithm requires the matrix to be square. Explain how to represent this problem as a square matrix. [2]

(iii) Use the Hungarian algorithm, reducing columns first, to pair the pupils to the positions. [5]

2 Two fencers have to decide on their strategies for a final. Neither knows what the other will do. The probabilities of Rani winning with each combination of tactics is as shown in the figure.

			Carl	
		X	Y	Z
	A	0.5	0.2	0.7
Rani	B	0.2	0.3	0.4
	C	0.6	0.4	0.5

(i) Explain why this is a 'zero-sum' game. [1]

(ii) Explain why Rani should never adopt strategy B. [1]

(iii) Which strategy should Carl never use? [1]

(iv) Reduce the table to a 2×2 pay-off matrix. Find the play-safe strategies for each fencer. [3]

(v) Which strategy would you advise Rani to play? Explain your answer. [2]

3 A mini-pack of breakfast cereals contains one packet of each of Chocbitz, Flakies, Oathearts, Ricebix and Swissmix. Anita likes Flakies and Ricebix, Bob only likes Flakies, Claudia likes Chocbitz and Swissmix, Damian likes Chocbitz, Oathearts and Ricebix, while Elvira likes Chocbitz, Oathearts and Swissmix.

(i) Show this information on a bipartite graph, G.   [2]

Anita chooses Flakies, Claudia the Chocbitz, Damian the Ricebix and Elvira the Swissmix. Bob is then disappointed.

(ii) Show the incomplete matching, M, that describes this choice of cereals.   [1]

(iii) Use a matching algorithm to construct an alternating path for M in G.   [3]

(iv) Hence find a maximal matching between the cereals and the students.   [2]

4   (i) Set up stage and state variables for the following diagram.   [2]

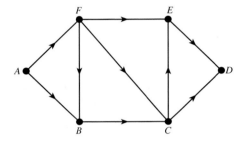

It is required to find the shortest route from A to D in the diagram.

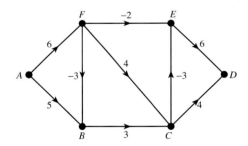

(ii) Explain why Dijkstra's method is not an appropriate method for this problem.   [1]

(iii) Set up and use a dynamic programming tabulation to find the shortest route from A to D.   [6]

(iv) What disadvantage does dynamic programming have compared to Dijkstra's algorithm?   [1]

5 The work needed to renovate a house has been divided into tasks, as shown in the table.

	Task	Duration (days)	Immediate predecessors	Worker
A	Construction	4	–	Bob
B	Rewiring preparation	1.5	A	Sparky
C	Plumbing preparation	2	A	Pip
D	Plastering	3	B, C	Art
E	Rewiring	0.5	D	Sparky
F	Plumbing	1	D	Pip
G	Joinery	2	E, F	Chip
H	Painting	3	G	Dec
I	Tiling	0.5	G	Tilly

(i) Construct an activity network for this project. [2]

(ii) Find the earliest and latest start times for each task. [4]

(iii) Identify the critical path and state the shortest completion time for the renovation. [2]

The developer is prepared to pay bonuses to speed up the work. The times for the rewiring could be reduced by 30%, for plumbing by 25% and for joinery by 25%.

(iv) To which workers should the developer offer bonuses? Justify your answers and find the new shortest completion time. [4]

6 The first diagram shows a system of pipes and the capacities, in litres per second, that each pipe can carry. The second diagram shows an initial flow.

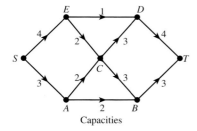
Capacities

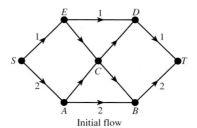
Initial flow

(i) Draw a diagram showing excess capacities and potential backflows. [4]

(ii) Augment your solution to part (i), using the labelling procedure and showing your working clearly, to find the maximum flow from S to T. [4]

(iii) Use the maximum flow–minimum cut theorem to verify that your answer to part (ii) is maximal. [2]

It is now given that node C has an upper capacity of 2 litres per second.

(iv) Show how the original diagram of capacities can be modified into a form to which you could apply the maximum flow–minimum cut theorem. [2]

(v) Hence prove that the restriction at C reduces the maximum flow from the value found in part (ii). [2]

Practice examination 2

Time 1 hour 20 minutes

Answer all the questions.

You are permitted to use a graphic calculator in this paper.

1 Apply the Hungarian algorithm, reducing rows first, to find the minimum possible total of four numbers, chosen from the table below in such a way that no two numbers lie in the same row or column. [6]

4	2	3	2
3	5	6	6
2	4	4	4
1	2	5	3

2 A garage has five mechanics who must be assigned to five different repairs.

> Val can repair clutches and engines;
> Will can repair clutches, dynamos and engines;
> Xi can repair accelerators and brakes;
> Yana can repair dynamos and engines;
> Zena can repair accelerators and dynamos.

(i) Draw a bipartite graph, G, to show which mechanic can repair which problem. [1]

The foreman decides to give the engine repair to Val, the clutch to Will, the accelerator to Xi and the dynamo to Zena. This leaves Yana without a suitable task.

(ii) Show the incomplete matching, M, that describes which task has been assigned to which mechanic. [1]

(iii) Use a matching algorithm to construct an alternating path for M in G, and hence find a maximal matching between the tasks and the mechanics. [4]

3 The diagram shows three stages in a manufacturing process. The nodes are labelled using (stage, state) and the values on the arcs represent times in hours.

Set up a dynamic programming tabulation to find the route for which the maximum time is a minimum (the minimax route). [10]

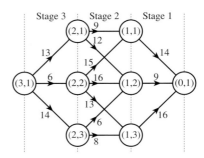

4 The initial stages of a major construction project are being planned. The table shows the tasks involved, their durations in weeks and their immediate predecessors.

	Task	Duration (weeks)	Immediate predecessors
A	Complete survey	5	–
B	Purchase land	24	A
C	Purchase materials	6	–
D	Hire machinery	4	–
E	Excavate foundations	4	B, D
F	Build access roads	5	B, C, D
G	Lay drains	4	E, F
H	Lay foundations	2	G

  (i) Draw an activity network for this project. [2]

 (ii) Given that the project is to be completed as soon as possible, find the earliest and latest starting time for each task.

  Give the fastest completion time and the critical path. [6]

Each of the tasks B, E, F, G can be speeded up at extra cost, as shown in the table.

	Task			
	B	E	F	G
Number of weeks by which the task can be speeded up	3	2	2	1
Extra cost per week of shortening (£1000s)	10	50	20	20

(iii) By how many weeks can the project be speeded up? Which tasks are speeded up and by how much? What will be the total extra cost? [3]

5 The figure shows a system of pipes with the lower and upper capacities, in litres per second, for each pipe.

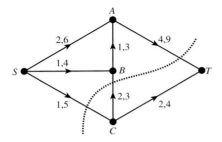

(i) Find the maximum value of the cut through arcs *SC, CB* and *AT* shown in the figure. [2]

(ii) Draw the network with a flow equal to the value of the cut found in part (i). Explain why this flow is a maximum. [3]

A pipe is added from *B* to *T* with lower and upper capacities of 0 and 5 litres per second respectively.

(iii) Augment your solution to part (ii), using the labelling procedure and showing your working clearly, to find the maximum flow from *S* to *T* for the new network. [5]

(iv) Find a minimum cut for the new network. [2]

6 Raj and Carla play a two-person zero-sum simultaneous-play game. The table shows the pay-off matrix for the game. The values in the table are the amounts won by Raj.

| | | Carla | |
		Strategy X	Strategy Y
Raj	Strategy A	−1	1
	Strategy B	3	−9

(i) Find the play-safe strategies for both Raj and Carla, and hence show that this game does not have a stable solution. [3]

(ii) Suppose that Raj knows that Carla will use her play-safe strategy. Explain whether or not he should change from his play-safe strategy as found in part (i). [1]

(iii) Suppose that Carla knows that Raj will use his play-safe strategy. Explain whether or not she should change from her play-safe strategy as found in part (i). [1]

Suppose that Carla uses random numbers to choose strategy X with probability p.

(iv) Show that the expected gain when Raj chooses strategy A is given by $1 - 2p$ and find a similar expression for the expected gain when Raj chooses his other strategy. [3]

(v) Use a graphical method to find the optimum value of p and the corresponding expected gain for Raj. [4]

(vi) Raj plays the game many times. What strategy should he use? Explain your answer. [3]

Answers

1 Matching

Exercise 1A (page 6)

1 (a)

The initial matching cannot be improved.

(b)

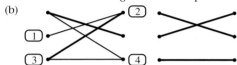

A complete matching is shown on the right.

2

$$\begin{array}{c c c c c} & R & S & T & U \\ A & \begin{pmatrix} 1 & 1 & 1 & 0 \\ B & 1 & 0 & 0 & 1 \\ C & 0 & 1 & 1 & 0 \\ D & 1 & 0 & 0 & 1 \end{pmatrix} \end{array}$$

A matching is $\{A, S\}, \{B, R\}, \{C, T\}, \{D, U\}$.
Others are possible.

3 (a,b)

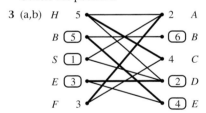

(c) S-D-E-E-B-B

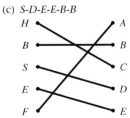

4 (a)

A •————————• Ah

B •————————• Ba

C •————————• Ch

D •————————• De

(b)

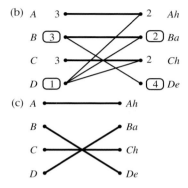

(c)

A •————————• Ah

B •   Ba

C •   Ch

D •   De

Exercise 1B (page 16)

1 (a) Add a column of 74s.
  (b) Back-E, Breast-D, Butterfly-A, Crawl-B.

2 (a) Subtract each element from 19.
  (b) Ali-Music, Bea-Sport. Chris-Science,
     Deepan-Literature.

3 $1 + 1 + 3 + 1 + 2 + 1 = 9$

4 23

5 (a) $5 \times 5 \times 2 - 3 \times 5 \times 2 = 20$
  (b) $(n - k)nl$

6 A-1, B-4, C-3, D-2

Miscellaneous exercise 1 (page 18)

1 (a,b)

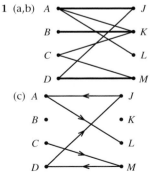

(c)

Arnold pairs with Lorna, Barry with Kate,
Charles with Marie, and Derek with Jane.

2 (a)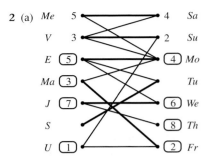

(b) *U-Fr-Ma-Mo-E-We-J-Th;*
Sa-Me, Su-V, Mo-Ma, Tu-S, We-E, Th-J,
Fr-U
Other solutions are possible.

3 (a)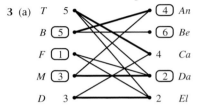

(b) *F-Da-M-An-B-Be*
Teddy bear - Cathy
Book - Ben
Football - Daniel
Money box - Annie
Drum - Elvis

4 (a,b)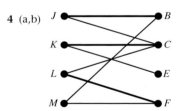

(c) *M-F-L-C-K-E;*
J-B, K-E, L-C, M-F
or
M-B-J-C-K-E;
J-C, K-E, L-F, M-B

5 (a) Jenny-Drainage, Kenny-Building,
Lenny-Carpentry, Penny-Electrics
(b) £14,000

6 (a) 1-*M*, 2-*L*, 3-*S*, 4-*T*
(b) £119,000

7 (a) Add a row of 0.51s.
(b)
$$\begin{pmatrix} \mathbf{0} & 0.02 & 0.02 & 0 & 0.06 \\ 0.02 & 0.05 & \mathbf{0} & 0.02 & 0.31 \\ 0.02 & \mathbf{0} & 0.02 & 0 & 0.38 \\ 0.02 & 0 & 0.01 & 0.03 & \mathbf{0} \\ 0.32 & 0.22 & 0.34 & \mathbf{0} & 0.32 \end{pmatrix}$$

An allocation of 5 zeros is now possible,
so this gives a minimum probability
allocation.
(c) *W-A, T-C, F-B, S-E*

8 Purple-Flowers, Orange-Diamonds,
Red-Gaudy, Yellow-Circles
or
Purple-Flowers, Orange-Gaudy, Red-Circles,
Yellow-Diamonds

9 (a) *W-C, T-A, F-E, S-B*
(b) £16.50

10 (a)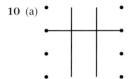

(b) For example, *A-T, B-U, C-S*.
(c) 3, because maximum matching =
minimum cover.

11 (a) Subtract all elements from 5.
(b) Add a row of 5s.
(c) *A-M, B-V, C-P, D-S, E-R*

12 (a) If the arc is in the matching, then see part
(d). If it is not in the matching, then any
labelling of the left-node would be
extended to one for the right-node.
(b) All left-nodes which do not belong to the
matching are labelled by Step 2 of the
algorithm.
(c) If a labelled right-node were not in the
matching, then the Matching
Augmentation algorithm could be used to
improve upon this maximal matching.
(d) If an arc of the matching has a labelled
right-node, then its left-node can be
labelled with a distance of at most 1 more.
If an arc of the matching has a labelled
left-node, then the labelling has to be
1 more than the labelling of the right-
node.

2 Network flows

Exercise 2A (page 25)

1 18, 20, 21, 24
The maximum flow is *at most* 18.

2 (a) 6   (b) Cut *SB, AB* and *AT*.

3 (a) 35 000   (b) *SC*

4 (a) Cut *CT, BT* and *AT* has value 21.
   (b) There is a flow of 21.

5 $k = 15$

Exercise 2B (page 32)

1

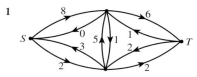

2

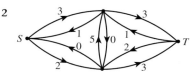

3 (a)

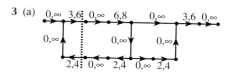

   (b) The cut shown above has value $6 - 2 = 4$.
      The maximum flow is 4.

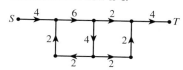

4

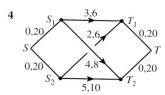

5 13 million

6 (a) Put all flows equal to the minimum
      capacities.
   (b) Augment by 4 *S-A-B-T* and 3 *S-C-T*.
      Total flow = 18.
   (c) Cut *CT* and *BT*.

7

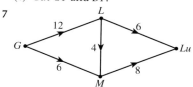

   Maximum flow = 14.

8 (a) $8 \leqslant$ flow $\leqslant 10$
   (b) $x \leqslant 10$, $y \geqslant 8$, $y \geqslant x$

9 (a) 40 000
   (b) Cut *M-E* and *Le-E*.

Miscellaneous exercise 2 (page 35)

1 (a) 560, 360
   (b) The maximum flow is at most 360. (It is
      actually 230.)

2 (a) Cut AC, *BC*, *DT* has value 22.
   (b) The established flow is only 19 whereas the
      maximum flow must be 22.
   (c) *S-A-D-B-C-T* of extra flow 3

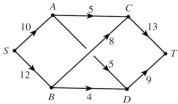

3 (a)

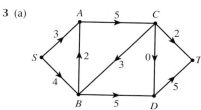

   (b) 11 litres per second

4 (a) $3 - 1 + 4 = 6$
   (b)

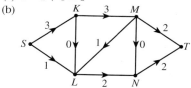

   (c) $4 \leqslant$ maximum flow $\leqslant 6$

5 (a) 32
   (b) Flow $\leqslant 32$.
   (d) *UW, VW, XW, XY, XZ* (plus possibly others)
      These arcs form a cut of value of 23 so the
      maximum flow is 23.

6 (a) 5. Cut *SA, BA* and *BT*.
      By the maximum flow–minimum cut
      theorem, the flow of 5 is maximal.
   (b) These represent 'flow in = flow out' for
      nodes *A* and *B*.
   (c) The objective function is the flow out of *S*.
      Alternatively use the flow into *T*, which is
      $x_{AT} + x_{BT}$.

7 (a) 5,4

(b)

	S	A, B, C, T	5
SA, SB			
SA, BC	S, B	A, C, T	4
AT, AC, SB	S, A	B, C, T	5
AT, AC, BC	S, A, B	C, T	4
SA, AC, CT	S, B, C	A, T	6
AT, CT	S, A, B, C	T	5

(c) 4000 vehicles per hour

8 (a) Join S_1, S_2 and S_3 to a single source S and T_1 and T_2 to a single sink T, with capacities of, say, 60.

(b) 40

(c)

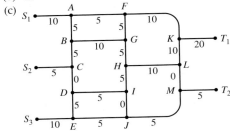

(d) (i) 30, by augmenting by 5 on S_2-C, C-D, D-I, I-J, J-M, M-T_2.
(ii) AF, AB, BC, CD, $S_3 E$ is a cut of 30, so by the maximum flow–minimum cut theorem the maximum is 30.

9 (a)

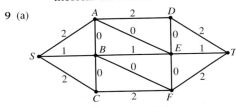

Other solutions are possible.
(b) Augment by 1 on S-B, B-E, E-T and 1 on S-C, C-B, B-A, A-E, E-D, D-T; 7.
(c) This is the maximum flow, because there is a cut of 7, AD, DE, ET, FT.

10 (a) Replace C by an arc from C_1 to C_2 with maximum capacity 10 and minimum 5 from C_1 to C_2. AC and BC are replaced by AC_1 and BC_1 and CD and CE are replaced by $C_2 D$ and $C_2 E$.
(b) $4 - 2 + 4 + 6 + 2 = 14$
(c) The maximum flow is less than or equal to 14. (It is actually 11.)

3 Critical path analysis

In this chapter there is not room to give the answers in the form of the examples in the text.

Exercise 3A (page 44)

1 (a)

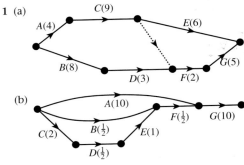

(b)

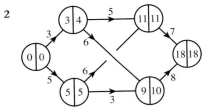

2

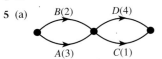

3 (a) From left to right. $(0\,|\,0)$, $(4\,|\,4)$, $(8\,|\,10)$. $(13\,|\,13)$, $(13\,|\,13)$, $(15\,|\,15)$, $(20\,|\,20)$.
(b) From left to right, $(0\,|\,0)$, $(2\,|\,8)$, $(2\frac{1}{2}\,|\,8\frac{1}{2})$. $(3\frac{1}{2}\,|\,9\frac{1}{2})$, $(10\,|\,10)$, $(20\,|\,20)$

4 17

5 (a)

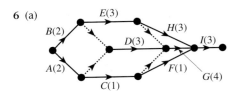

(b)

Activity	A	B	C	D
Early	0	0	3	3
Late	0	1	6	3

6 (a)

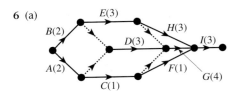

(b)
Activity	A	B	C	D	E	F	G	H	I
Early	0	0	2	2	2	3	5	5	9
Late	1	0	4	3	2	8	5	6	9

Exercise 3B (page 47)

1 *ABHI*

2 Activity *I* because it is the only one which is critical.

3 (a) From left to right, (0 | 0), (3 | 3), (7 | 7), (10 | 10)

(b) (0 | 0), (3 | 3), (6 | 6), (9 | 9)

$t \geqslant 3$

4 (a)
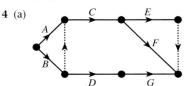

(b)
Activity	A	B	C	D	E	F	G
Early	0	0	5	5	13	13	8
Late	3	0	5	9	13	14	12

(c) *BCE*, 15 days   (d) *BDG*

5 (a)
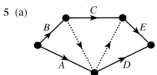

From left to right, (0 | 0), (2 | 4), (5 | 5), (5 | 5), (8 | 8)

(b) 8 days; *A, E*

6 (a)
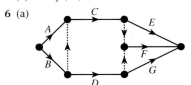

(b) *BCE*, 11 weeks   (c) *F*, by 3 weeks

7 (a) *AD*, 8 days   (b) 5 days

Exercise 3C (page 53)

1 (a) 20 hours; *B, C, E, G*

(b)
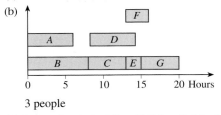

3 people

(c) Delay the start of *F* until *D* has finished.

2 (a)
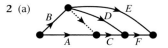

(b) *BE*, 6 days

(c) People
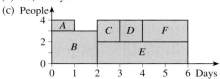

3 (a) *AFG*, 30 days

Start times:
Activity	A	B	C	D	E	F	G
Early	0	0	3	3	12	12	24
Late	0	3	8	6	18	12	24

Finish times:
Activity	A	B	C	D	E	F	G
Early	12	3	7	9	18	24	30
Late	12	6	12	12	24	24	30

(b) 3

(c) 1 day, Run *C* and *D* one after the other.

4 (a)
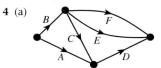

BE, 26 days

(b) People
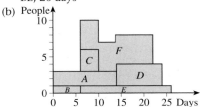

(c) Delay *F* to start after activity *C*.

Miscellaneous exercise 3 (page 54)

1 (a)
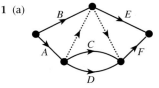

(b) 10 days; *B, E, F*   (c) £1250

2 (a)
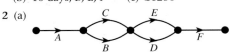

The early and late times reading from the left are (0 | 0), (5 | 5), (7 | 7), (11 | 11), (12 | 12).

(b) The earliest and latest start times for the activities are $A(0, 0)$, $B(5, 5)$, $C(5, 6)$, $D(7, 9)$, $E(7, 7)$, $F(11, 11)$.

(c) *ABEF*, 12 hours

(d) *E* now has an effective duration of 5 hours. The critical path is 1 hour longer.

3 (a)

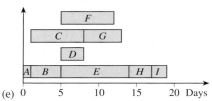

The early and late times reading from the left are $(0 \mid 0)$, $(1 \mid 1)$, $(5 \mid 5)$, $(14 \mid 14)$, $(8 \mid 11)$, $(17 \mid 17)$, $(19 \mid 19)$.

(b,c)
Activity	A	B	C	D	E	F	G	H	I
Early start	0	1	1	5	5	5	8	14	17
Late finish	1	5	11	11	14	17	17	17	19

(d) *ABEHI*, 19 days

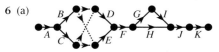

(f) People ↑

(g) For example, delay the start of *F* for 3 days.

4 (a)

The early and late times reading from the left are $(0 \mid 0)$, $(3 \mid 4)$, $(4 \mid 4)$, $(5 \mid 6)$, $(7 \mid 7)$, $(7 \mid 11)$, $(11 \mid 12)$, $(14 \mid 14)$, $(14 \mid 16)$, $(20 \mid 20)$, $(23 \mid 23)$.

(b,c)
Act.	A	B	C	D	E	F	G	H	I	J	K
E. s.	0	0	3	4	7	5	7	14	14	11	20
L. f.	4	4	6	7	16	12	14	20	20	20	23

(d) *BDGIK*, 23 weeks

(e) (i) Speed up *I* by 2 weeks since it is on the critical path, Leave *E* as it is not on the critical path. Speed up *J* since it is now

on the critical path. Only 1 week is relevant.

(ii) 21 weeks

(iii) £11,000

5 (a)

(b)
Activity	A	B	C	D	E	F	G	H	I	J
Early start	0	0	7	7	5	5	10	12	13	22
Late start	0	4	7	9	13	9	18	16	13	22

(c) The slack times are A 0, B 4, C 0, D 2, E 8, F 4, G 8, H 4, I 0, J 0; *ACIJ*, 25 days

6 (a)

(b)
Act.	A	B	C	D	E	F	G	H	I	J	K
E. s.	0	3	3	9	9	15	17	17	18	20	26
L. s.	0	3	4	11	9	15	18	17	19	20	26

(c) *ABEFHJK*, 27 days

(d) *G* and *I* become critical instead of *H*, saving 1 day.

7 (a)

(b)
Activity	A	B	C	D	E	F
Early start	0	0	3	2	4	8
Late start	0	1	3	3	4	8

(c) *A, C, E, F*; 13 days

(d) Six people will be required for each of four days between days 2 and 8. Four of these people will do *D*, and the remainder whichever of *A*, *C* and *E* is going on in parallel.

8 (a)

(b)
Activity	A	B	C	D	E	F	G	H	I
Early start	0	0	45	57	45	59	59	62	63
Late start	0	39	45	57	55	59	61	62	63

(c) *ACDFHI*, 66 days

(d) 10 days

9 (a)

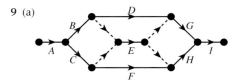

(b)

Activity	A	B	C	D	E	F	G	H	I
Early start	0	5	5	7	9	9	13	13	16
Late start	0	7	5	9	9	10	14	13	16

(c) *ACEHI*, 20 days

10 (a)

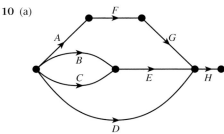

(b) 22 minutes   (c) *D, H*   (d) 32 minutes

4 Dynamic programming

Exercise 4A (page 66)

1 *A*(5, 1), *B*(3, 1), *C*(2, 1), *D*(0, 1), *E*(1, 1), *F*(4, 1)

2 *AEBCD*, 6 lights

3 (a) *AGCE*, 17 miles   (b) *ABCDE*, £26,000

4 (a) There are negative weights.
   (b) *AFBCED*, 7

5 From *A*, *ADGJMN*, 13
   From *B*, *BDGJMN*, 12
   From *C*, *CHJMN*, 10

Exercise 4B (page 70)

1 (a) Minimax   (b) Minimising   (c) Maximin
   (d) Minimax   (e) Maximin (speeds)

2 (a)

Stage	State	Act.	Value	Maximum
1	1	1	5	← 5
	2	1	4	← 4
2	1	1	6 + 5 = 11	← 11
		2	7 + 4 = 11	
	2	1	8 + 5 = 13	← 13
		2	3 + 4 = 7	
3	1	1	1 + 11 = 12	
		2	2 + 13 = 15	← 15

(3, 1), (2, 2), (1, 1), (0, 1); 15

(b)

Stage	State	Act.	Value	Minimum
1	1	1	5	← 5
	2	1	4	← 4
2	1	1	6 + 5 = 11	← 11
		2	7 + 4 = 11	
	2	1	8 + 5 = 13	
		2	3 + 4 = 7	← 7
3	1	1	1 + 11 = 12	
		2	2 + 7 = 9	← 9

(3, 1), (2, 2), (1, 2), (0, 1); 9

(c)

Stage	State	Act.	Value	Maximum
1	1	1	5	← 5
	2	1	4	← 4
2	1	1	min(6, 5) = 5	← 5
		2	min(7, 4) = 4	
	2	1	min(8, 5) = 5	← 5
		2	min(3,4) = 3	
3	1	1	min(1, 5) = 1	
		2	min(2, 5) = 2	← 2

(3, 1), (2, 2), (1, 1), (0, 1); 2

(d)

Stage	State	Act.	Value	Minimax
1	1	1	5	← 5
	2	1	4	← 4
2	1	1	max(6, 5) = 6	← 6
		2	max(7, 4) = 7	
	2	1	max(8, 5) = 8	
		2	max(3, 4) = 4	← 4
3	1	1	max(1, 6) = 6	
		2	max(2, 4) = 4	← 4

(3, 1), (2, 2), (1, 2), (0, 1); 4

3 8 tonnes (*ACFG*)

4 4 hours (*ABCFE*)

5 (a) 6
   (b) It must contain an action of cost 6 or less.

6 (a) max(*a,c*)
   (b) min(*b,d*)
   (c) (i)

Maximin = 1
Minimax = 2

Other solutions are possible.

(ii)

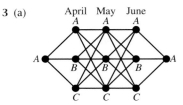

Maximin = 3
Minimax = 2

Other solutions are possible.

7 (a) (3, 1), (2, 3), (1, 3), (0,1); 4
  (b) (3, 1), (2, 1), (1, 1), (0,1); 4

Miscellaneous exercise 4 (page 72)

1

Stage	State	Act.	Value	Maximin
1	1	1	3	← 3
	2	1	4	← 4
	3	1	6	← 6
2	1	1	min(4, 3) = 3	
		2	min(4, 4) = 4	← 4
	2	1	min(5, 3) = 3	
		2	min(2, 4) = 2	
		3	min(4, 6) = 4	← 4
	3	1	min(3, 4) = 3	
		2	min(5, 6) = 5	← 5
3	1	1	min(6, 4) = 4	
		2	min(3, 4) = 3	
		3	min(6, 5) = 5	← 5

(3, 1), (2, 3), (1, 3), (0, 1); maximin = 5

2

Stage	State	Act.	Value	Maximum
1	1	1	3	← 3
	2	1	4	← 4
	3	1	5	← 5
2	1	1	6 + 3 = 9	← 9
		2	5 + 4 = 9	← 9
	2	1	5 + 3 = 8	
		2	5 + 4 = 9	← 9
		3	3 + 5 = 8	
	3	1	6 + 4 = 10	← 10
		2	4 + 5 = 9	
3	1	1	3 + 9 = 12	
		2	6 + 9 = 15	← 15
		3	4 + 10 = 14	

(3, 1), (2, 2), (1, 2), (0, 1); maximum = £15

3 (a)

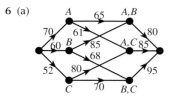

April May June
A   A   A

A

B   B   B

C   C   C

(b) £186   (c) April-C, May-C, June-A; £154

4 (a) Dijkstra's algorithm is of quadratic order
   compared to the cubic order of the
   dynamic programming solution. Dijkstra's
   algorithm will therefore be much quicker
   for larger problems.
  (b) Dijkstra's algorithm cannot be used if some
   arcs have negative weights whereas
   dynamic programming can.

5 (a) (i)

Stage	State	Act.	Value	Minimum
1	1	1	8	← 8
	2	1	6	← 6
	3	1	10	← 10
2	1	1	11 + 8 = 19	
		2	6 + 6 = 12	← 12
	2	1	9 + 6 = 15	
		2	4 + 10 = 14	← 14
3	1	1	3 + 12 = 15	← 15
		2	2 + 14 = 16	
	2	1	13 + 14 = 27	
		2	5 + 10 = 15	← 15
4	1	1	6 + 15 = 21	← 21
		1	8 + 15 = 23	

  SABET, 21

  (ii) There is a cut of value 13, *AB*, *AD*, *SF*.
   There is also a flow of 13: *SA* 5, *SF* 8,
   AB 3, *AD* 2, *FD* 3, *FG* 5, *BC* 3, *BE* 0,
   DE 5, *DG* 0, *CT* 3, *ET* 5, *GT* 5; so this
   flow is maximal.
  (iii) *SFDET*, 36 days
  (b) Network (iii); maximum profit = £36,000

6 (a)

A   65   A,B
70   61   80
  60 B   85   A,C 85
          68
52   80   95
       C   70   B,C

(b) (i) *A, B, C*; £21,500,000
 (ii) *A, B, C*; £8,000,000
 (iii) *A, B, C*; £6,500,000

(c) Reduce it to any amount less than
£7,000,000. The routes are then
(i) *C, B, A*   (ii) *B, C, A*   (iii) *A, B, C*

7 (a)

Stage	State	Act.	Value	Minimum
1	1	1	13	← 13
	2	1	7	← 7
2	1	1	25 + 13 = 38	
		2	28 + 7 = 35	← 35
	2	1	19 + 13 = 32	
		2	22 + 7 = 29	← 29
	3	1	37 + 13 = 50	
		2	22 + 7 = 29	← 29
3	1	1	10 + 35 = 45	
		2	17 + 29 = 46	
		3	13 + 29 = 42	← 42

(b) *SCET*, 42

(c) An advantage is that dynamic
programming can deal with negative
numbers on the arcs; a disadvantage is that
it has higher polyomial order and so takes
longer for large problems.

8 13 cakes, costing £78 must be baked. Remove
this from the table, and add later.

Day	State	Make	Store	D. cost	Total
Fri.	0	2	0	2.5	2.5 ←
	1	1	0	2.5	2.5 ←
	2	0	0	0	0 ←
Thu.	0	4	1	3	5.5
		3	0	2.5	5 ←
	1	4	2	3.5	3.5 ←
		3	1	3	5.5
		2	0	2.5	5
	2	3	2	3.5	3.5 ←
		2	1	3	5.5
		1	0	2.5	5
	3	2	2	3.5	3.5
		1	1	3	5.5
		0	0	0	2.5 ←

Day	State	Make	Store	D. cost	Total
Wed.	1	4	0	2.5	7.5 ←
	2	4	1	3	6.5 ←
		3	0	2.5	7.5
	3	4	2	3.5	7
		3	1	3	6.5 ←
		2	0	2.5	7.5
Tue.	0	4	2	3.5	10 ←
		3	1	3	10.5
	1	4	3	4	10.5
		3	2	3.5	10 ←
		2	1	3	10.5
	2	3	3	4	10.5
		2	2	3.5	10 ←
		1	1	3	10.5
	3	2	3	4	10.5
		1	2	3.5	10
		0	1	0.5	8 ←
Mon.	0	4	3	4	12 ←
		3	2	3.5	13.5
		2	1	3	13
		1	0	2.5	12.5

Make 4, 0, 4, 3, 2, store 3, 1, 0, 0, 0,
costing £90.

9

Stage	State	Act.	Value	Minimax
1	1	1	4	← 4
	2	1	6	← 6
	3	1	5	← 5
2	1	1	max(3, 4) = 4	← 4
		2	max(5, 6) = 6	
	2	1	max(2, 6) = 6	
		2	max(1, 5) = 5	← 5
	3	1	max(2, 6) = 6	
		2	max(3, 5) = 5	← 5
3	1	1	max(4, 4) = 4	← 4
		2	max(3, 5) = 5	
		3	max(4, 5) = 5	

(3, 1), (2, 1), (1, 1), (0, 1); 4

10

Stage	State	Act.	Value	Minimum
1	1	0	5	← 5
	2	1	3	← 3
2	1	0	$6 + 5 = 11$	
		1	$2 + 3 = 5$	← 5
	2	0	$3 + 5 = 8$	← 8
		1	$6 + 3 = 9$	
3	1	0	$3 + 5 = 8$	← 8
		1	$3 + 8 = 11$	
	2	0	$5 + 5 = 10$	← 10
		1	$3 + 8 = 11$	
4	1	0	$5 + 8 = 13$	← 13
		1	$4 + 10 = 14$	

The route is (4, 1), (3, 1), (2, 1), (1, 2), (0, 1); 13.

11

Stage	State	Act.	Value	Maximum
1	1	1	3	← 3
	2	1	4	← 4
	3	1	5	← 5
2	1	1	$6 + 3 = 9$	← 9
	2	1	$5 + 3 = 8$	
		2	$5 + 4 = 9$	
		3	$5 + 5 = 10$	← 10
	3	1	$6 + 4 = 10$	
		2	$6 + 5 = 11$	← 11
3	1	1	$4 + 9 = 13$	
		2	$4 + 10 = 14$	← 14
	2	1	$3 + 9 = 12$	
		2	$3 + 10 = 13$	← 13
	3	1	$2 + 10 = 12$	
		2	$2 + 11 = 13$	← 13

Visit (0, 1), (1, 3), (2, 2), (3, 1); £14,000

5 Game theory

Exercise 5A (page 82)

1 $\begin{pmatrix} -3 & 2 & -1 & 2 \\ -1 & 1 & 0 & -1 \\ 2 & -4 & -2 & 3 \end{pmatrix}$

2 (a) A1, B2, 4   (b) A2, B2, 3
   (c) A1, B4, −2   (d) A1, B2, −3

3 (a) Yes, value 4   (b) Yes, value 3
   (c) No   (d) No

4 (a) Yes   (b) No
   (c) Yes   (d) Yes

5 A3, B3. The game has a stable solution so neither player can improve their pay-off.

6 (a) It is dominated by strategy number 2.
   (b) Y
   (c) $\begin{pmatrix} 0.2 & 0.1 \\ 0.3 & 0.6 \end{pmatrix}$, United 2, City X
   (d) Strategy number 2 as the solution is stable.

Exercise 5B (page 88)

1 (a) $X: 1 + 2p; Y: 3 - 5p; Z: 2 - p$
   (b) $\frac{2}{7}$ (c) Ann $\frac{11}{7}$, Ben $-\frac{11}{7}$
   (d) Strategy Z

2 (a) $3 + 2p, 4 - 2p$
   (b) $2 + 3q, 4 - q$
   (c) $\frac{7}{2}; \frac{1}{4}, \frac{1}{2}$

3 (a) $\frac{17}{5}$ (b) $\frac{5}{3}$ (c) $\frac{5}{7}$

4 (a) $\begin{pmatrix} 6 & 2 \\ 1 & 5 \end{pmatrix}$ (b) $\frac{7}{2}$

5 Mixture is dominated by New.
   (a) $8 - 7p, 5 - 2p, 3 + 5p$
   (b)

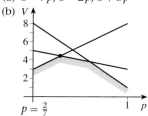

Exercise 5C (page 92)

1 Maximise v,
   subject to $v \leqslant 4p + 3q$,
   $v \leqslant p + 5q$,
   $p + q \leqslant 1$,
   $p, q \geqslant 0$.

P	v	p	q	r	s	t	
1	−1	0	0	0	0	0	0
0	0	1	1	1	0	0	1
0	**1**	−4	−3	0	1	0	0
0	1	−1	−5	0	0	1	0
1	0	−4	−3	0	1	0	0
0	0	1	1	1	0	0	1
0	1	−4	−3	0	1	0	0
0	0	**3**	−2	0	−1	1	0
1	0	0	$-\frac{17}{3}$	0	$-\frac{1}{3}$	$\frac{4}{3}$	0
0	0	0	$\frac{5}{3}$	1	$\frac{1}{3}$	$-\frac{1}{3}$	1
0	1	0	$-\frac{17}{3}$	0	$-\frac{1}{3}$	$\frac{4}{3}$	0
0	0	1	$-\frac{2}{3}$	0	$-\frac{1}{3}$	$\frac{1}{3}$	0
1	0	0	0	$\frac{17}{5}$	$\frac{4}{5}$	$\frac{1}{5}$	$\frac{17}{5}$
0	0	0	1	$\frac{3}{5}$	$\frac{1}{5}$	$-\frac{1}{5}$	$\frac{3}{5}$
0	1	0	0	$\frac{17}{5}$	$\frac{4}{5}$	$\frac{1}{5}$	$\frac{17}{5}$
0	0	1	0	$\frac{2}{5}$	$-\frac{1}{5}$	$\frac{1}{5}$	$\frac{2}{5}$

$v = \frac{17}{5}; p = \frac{2}{5}, q = \frac{3}{5}$

2 Maximise $v - 2$,
subject to $v \le p + 4q$,
$v \le 5p + q$,
$p + q \le 1$,
$p, q \ge 0$.
$v = \frac{5}{7}$

3 Maximise v,
subject to $v \le 3p + 4q + 2r$
$v \le 2p + 5q + 4r$
$v \le 5p + 2q + 4r$
$p + q + r \le 1$
$p, q, r \ge 0$.

Miscellaneous exercise 5 (page 92)

1 max(row min) = min(col max) = 1
Both play option 2.

2 (a) $1 - p - 2q, 2p + q - 1, q - p$
(b) By choosing $p = q = 1 - p - q = \frac{1}{3}$
(c) 0. Each player can guarantee this by choosing their options with equal probabilities.

3 (a) max(row min) = −2 and min(col max) = 1; these are unequal so the game does not have a stable solution.
(b) (i) 1 (ii) −0.8 (iii) 0.1
(c) A plays 1 with probability $\frac{3}{8}$; the pay-off is $-\frac{1}{8}$.

4 (a) Roland plays S, gain ≥ -1, and Colleen plays S, loss ≤ 3. As these outcomes are unequal, the game does not have a stable solution.
(b) (i) T (ii) S
(c) $5p - 2$
(d)

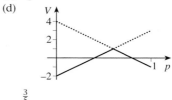

$\frac{3}{5}$

5 (a) Atomic energy is dominated by Bio-gas, and Windy is dominated by Wet.
(b) max(row min) = 2 and min(col max) = 4; these are unequal so the game does not have a stable solution.
(c) $1 + 3p$ (d) $\frac{2}{3}, 3$

6 (a) P and B; max (row min) = −1 and min(col max) = 1; these are unequal so the game does not have a stable solution.
(b) (i) P (ii) A
(c) $3 - 4p$ (d) $\frac{7}{9}, \frac{1}{9}$

7 (a) Rowena: B, guarantees ≥ 3, Colin: Z, guarantees ≤ 3; these are equal, so the game has a stable solution.
(b) There is no advantage to either player in varying from play-safe strategy.
(c) X is dominated by Z;
C is dominated by B or A is dominated by B.

	Y	Z
A	−1	2
B	6	3

or

	Y	Z
B	6	3
C	2	−2

(d) $2 - 3p, 3 + 3p$ (e) $0, -3$

8 (a) Zero-sum game means that the gain of one player added to the gain of the other player is zero.
(b) Richard: A, gain ≥ -2;
Carol: Z, loss ≤ 1;
these are unequal so the game does not have a stable solution.
(c) Richard will change to C.
(d) Carol will not change.

9 (a) Rose: Hide, gain ≥ 3;
Computer: Shoot, loss ≤ 4; these are unequal so the game does not have a stable solution.

(b) It is dominated by both of the other strategies.

(c) Track, because it is dominated by Shoot.

(d) Computer chooses Shoot, gain $5p - 1$; computer chooses Fight, gain $5 - 2p$.

(e) $\frac{6}{7}$

10 (a) Elf is dominated by Dragon.

(b) Crystal

(c) New matrix is

	D	F
A	0.4	0.3
B	0.5	0.8

Richard: Bronze, expected gain 0.5; Computer: Dragon, expected gain to Richard 0.5.

(d) The game has a stable solution, so Richard should always play Bronze.

Revison exercise (page 97)

1 (a)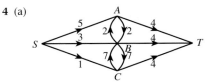

A   3   2   E

B   3   2   F

C   ③   ②   G

D   ①   ④   H

(b) A ———— E

B ———— F

C ⤬ G

D ⤬ H

2 (a)
Activity	A	B	C	D	E	F	G	H	I
Early start	0	0	2	3	3	3	5	5	8
Late start	1	0	2	5	3	4	6	5	8
Early finish	1	2	3	4	5	4	7	8	9
Late finish	2	2	3	6	5	5	8	8	9
Float	1	0	0	2	0	1	1	0	0

(b) 9 days

(c) B, C, E, H, I

(d) It need have no effect because G has a float of 1 day.

3 (a) For example, replace all scores by '$8 - score$'.

(b) Add a row of equal scores.

(c) L-W, M-X, N-Y or L-Z, M-X, N-W

4 (a)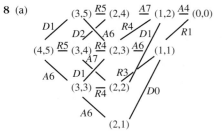

(b) A cut is any continuous line which separates S from T. It must not pass through any nodes.

(c) 8

(d)
X	Y	Value
S	T, A, B, C	9
S, A	T, B, C	10
S, B	T, A, C	19
S, C	T, A, B	19
S, A, B	T, C	16
S, A, C	T, B	17
S, B, C	T, A	15
S, A, B, C	T	12

(e) The maximum possible flow is 9.

5 (a) SDCT, SDBCT, SDBT, SADCT, SADBCT, SADBT, SABCT, SABT

(b) C_1: 340; C_2: 250. The maximum flow is at most 250 people per hour.

(c) 200 people per hour

6 (a)
Activity	A	B	C	D	E	F	G	H	I	J
Early start	0	2	2	2	2	4	3	7	8	18
Late start	0	13	10	2	2	4	3	15	8	18
Early finish	2	4	7	4	3	8	8	10	18	22
Late finish	2	15	15	4	3	8	8	18	18	22

(b) A, D, E, F, G, I, J

(c) Delay the start of C until day 8. Delay the start of H until day 13.

7 1-A, 2-B, 3-C, 4-D or 1-C, 2-B, 3-A, 4-D or 1-C, 2-B, 3-D, 4-A

8 (a)

$(3,5) \xrightarrow{R5} (2,4) \xrightarrow{A7} (1,2) \xrightarrow{A4} (0,0)$

D1   D2 ⤬ A6   R4 ⤬ D1   R1

$(4,5) \xrightarrow{R5} (3,4) \xrightarrow{R4} (2,3) \xrightarrow{A6} (1,1)$

A6   D1 ⤬ R3

$(3,3) \xrightarrow{R4} (2,2)$ D0

A6 $(2,1)$

(b)

Stage	State	Action	Cost
1	1	R	1 ←
	2	A	4 ←
2	1	D	$1 + 0 = 1$ ←
	2	R	$1 + 3 = 4$
		D	$4 + 1 = 5$ ←
	3	A	$1 + 6 = 7$
		R	$4 + 4 = 8$ ←
	4	A	$4 + 7 = 11$ ←
3	3	A	$1 + 6 = 7$
		R	$5 + 4 = 9$ ←
		D	$8 + 1 = 9$ ←
3	4	A	$5 + 7 = 12$
		R	$8 + 4 = 12$
		D	$11 + 2 = 13$ ←
3	5	A	$8 + 6 = 14$
		R	$11 + 5 = 16$ ←
4	5	A	$9 + 6 = 15$
		R	$13 + 5 = 18$ ←
		D	$16 + 1 = 17$

The best strategy is 1: Run, 2: Dodge, 3: Attack, 4: Attack.
The number of squares is 18.

9 (a) (3, 1), (2, 2), (1, 2), (0, 1); 7
   (b) (3, 1), (2, 3), (1, 3), (0, 1); 14

10 (a) Maximise $v - 6$,
   subject to $v \leqslant 8p_1 + 2p_2 + p_3$,
   $v \leqslant 9p_1 + 5p_2 + 6p_3$,
   $v \leqslant 4p_1 + 5p_2 + 7p_3$,
   $p_1 + p_2 + p_3 \leqslant 1$,
   $p_1, p_2, p_3 \geqslant 0$.

(b)

P	v	p_1	p_2	p_3	r	s	t	u	
1	−1	0	0	0	0	0	0	0	−6
0	1	−8	−2	−1	1	0	0	0	0
0	1	−9	−5	−6	0	1	0	0	0
0	1	−4	−5	−7	0	0	1	0	0
0	0	1	1	1	0	0	0	1	1

11

Stage	State	Action	Profit
1	1	B	1
		C	3 ←
	2	A	1
		B	2
		C	6 ←
	3	A	1
		B	2 ←
2	1	B	$2 + 3 = 5$
		C	$3 + 6 = 9$ ←
	2	A	$1 + 3 = 4$
		B	$3 + 6 = 9$ ←
		C	$6 + 2 = 8$
	3	A	$5 + 6 = 11$ ←
		B	$4 + 2 = 6$
3	1	A	$3 + 9 = 12$
		B	$4 + 9 = 13$
		C	$3 + 11 = 14$ ←

Profit is £14,000, by choosing C, A, C.

12 (a) His row is dominated by Minnie's.
   (b) 5, 6, 5.5
   (c) $6 - 2p, 5 + 2p, 7 - 3p$
   (d)

				Min	
Minnie	4	7	4	4	
Max	6	5	7	5	←

Max should play.

Practice examinations

Practice examination 1 (page 103)

1 (i) Subtract each element from, say, 8.
   (ii) Add another row of equal numbers, say 1s.
   (iii)

3	1	1	3	2		2	**0**	1	2	1
2	1	0	4	1		1	0	**0**	3	0
1	3	2	3	1	→	**0**	2	2	2	0
2	3	1	2	1		1	2	1	1	**0**
1	1	1	1	1		0	0	1	**0**	0

Head prefect - B, Captain of sports - C, Library prefect - A, Charities prefect - E.

2 (i) A win for Rani is a loss for Carl and vice versa.

(ii) It is dominated by C.

(iii) Z

(iv)

	X	Y
A	0.5	0.2
C	0.6	0.4

Rani: C, Carl: Y

(v) C; the solution is stable.

3 (i, ii, iii)

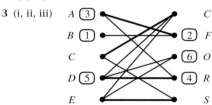

B-F-A-R-D-O

(iv) A-R, B-F, C-C, D-O, E-S

4 (i) $A(5, 1)$, $B(3, 1)$, $C(2, 1)$, $D(0, 1)$, $E(1, 1)$, $F(4, 1)$

(ii) There are negative weights.

(iii)

Stage	Action	Value	Minimum
E	1	6	$\leftarrow 6$
C	1	$-3 + 6 = 3$	$\leftarrow 3$
	2	4	
B	1	$3 + 3 = 6$	$\leftarrow 6$
F	1	$-2 + 6 = 4$	
	2	$4 + 3 = 7$	
	3	$-3 + 6 = 3$	$\leftarrow 3$
A	1	$6 + 3 = 9$	$\leftarrow 9$
	2	$5 + 6 = 11$	

A, F, B, C, E, D; 9

(iv) It has a higher polynomial order and therefore takes longer for large problems.

5 (i)

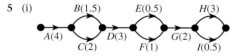

$B(1.5)$ $E(0.5)$ $H(3)$
$A(4)$ $C(2)$ $D(3)$ $F(1)$ $G(2)$ $I(0.5)$

(ii)

Activity	A	B	C	D	E	F	G	H	I
Early start	0	4	4	6	9	9	10	12	12
Late start	0	4.5	4	6	9.5	9	10	12	14.5

(iii) $ACDFGH$, 15 days

(iv) Sparky: no, B and E are not critical.

Pip: yes, reduces the time by $\frac{3}{4}$ day.

Chip: yes, reduces the time by $\frac{1}{2}$ day.

$13\frac{3}{4}$ days

6 (i)

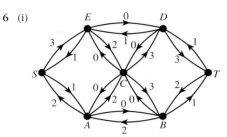

(ii) $SACBT$: 1, $SECDT$: 2, maximum flow $= 6$.

(iii) ED, EC, SA is a cut of value 6. So the flow of 6 is maximal.

(iv) Replace C by C_1 — 2 — C_2

(v) ED, C_1C_2, AB is a cut of value 5.

Practice examination 2 (page 106)

1
$$\begin{pmatrix} 2 & 0 & 1 & 0 \\ 0 & 2 & 3 & 3 \\ 0 & 2 & 2 & 2 \\ 0 & 1 & 4 & 2 \end{pmatrix} \rightarrow \begin{pmatrix} 2 & 0 & 0 & 0 \\ 0 & 2 & 2 & 3 \\ 0 & 2 & 1 & 2 \\ 0 & 1 & 3 & 2 \end{pmatrix} \rightarrow \begin{pmatrix} 3 & 0 & 0 & 0 \\ 0 & 1 & 1 & 2 \\ 0 & 1 & 0 & 1 \\ 0 & 0 & 2 & 1 \end{pmatrix}$$

The minimum total is $2 + 3 + 4 + 2 = 11$.

2 (i, ii, iii)

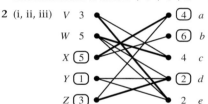

V 3 $\boxed{4}$ a
W 5 $\boxed{6}$ b
X $\boxed{5}$ 4 c
Y $\boxed{1}$ $\boxed{2}$ d
Z $\boxed{3}$ 2 e

Y-d-Z-a-X-b

V-e, W-c, X-b, Y-d, Z-a

3

Stage	State	Act.	Value	Minimax
1	1	1	14	$\leftarrow 14$
	2	1	9	$\leftarrow 9$
	3	1	16	$\leftarrow 16$
2	1	1	$\max(9, 14) = 14$	
		2	$\max(12, 9) = 12$	$\leftarrow 12$
	2	1	$\max(15, 14) = 15$	$\leftarrow 15$
		2	$\max(16, 9) = 16$	
		3	$\max(13, 16) = 16$	
	3	1	$\max(6, 9) = 9$	$\leftarrow 9$
		2	$\max(8, 16) = 16$	
3	1	1	$\max(13, 12) = 13$	$\leftarrow 13$
		2	$\max(6, 15) = 15$	
		3	$\max(14, 9) = 14$	

$(3, 1)$, $(2, 1)$, $(1, 2)$, $(0, 1)$; minimax $= 13$

4 (i)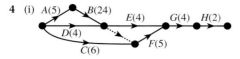

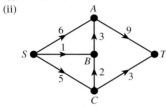

(ii)

Activity	A	B	C	D	E	F	G	H
Early start	0	5	0	0	29	29	34	38
Late start	0	5	23	25	30	29	34	38

40 weeks; *ABFGH*

(iii) 6 weeks; *B*-3, *E*-1, *F*-2, *G*-1
Cost £140,000

5 (i) $5 - 2 + 9 = 12$

(ii)

Flow = cut. Therefore flow is maximum by the maximum flow–minimum cut theorem.

(iii)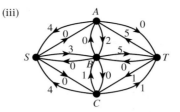

Augment *SBT* by 3.
Maximum flow = 15.

(iv) Cut *SA*, *SB* and *SC*.

6 (i) Raj: *A*, value $\geqslant -1$; Carla: *Y*, value $\leqslant 1$; these are unequal so the game does not have a stable solution.

(ii) Raj will not change.

(iii) Carla will change to *X*.

(iv) $-1 \times p + 1 \times (1 - p) = 1 - 2p, \ 12p - 9$

(v) $p = \frac{5}{7}, -\frac{3}{7}$

(vi) Choose *A* with probability $\frac{6}{7}$, *B* with probability $\frac{1}{7}$. The game then has value $-\frac{3}{7}$ irrespective of Carla's choice.

Glossary

Action	Arc of a dynamic programming network.
Activity network	Network which represents the splitting up of a major project into activities.
Allocation problem	Matching problem where total cost must be minimised.
Alternating path	Path from an unmatched left-node to an unmatched right-node which consists alternately of arcs not in the matching and arcs in the matching.
Capacities	Weights on arcs in network flow problems.
Cascade chart	Chart showing possible time slots of all activities involved in a project.
Complete matching	Matching which covers all nodes of a bipartite graph.
Critical path	Path through an activity network consisting only of critical activities which have no scheduling flexibility.
Cut	Continuous line separating the source (start node) from the sink (end node).
Dominance	Process of ignoring a particular choice of action in a two-person game when that choice is always inferior to another choice.
Float	Flexibility in scheduling an activity.
$m \times n$ game	Two-person zero-sum game where one player has m possible choices of action and the other player has n possible choices.
Matching	Set of arcs of a bipartite graph which have no nodes in common.
Maximin	Problem of finding a route which maximises minimum cost.
Minimax	Problem of finding a route which minimises maximum cost.
Pay-off matrix	Rectangular array of numbers representing outcomes of pairs of decisions.
Resource levelling	Smoothing out of the use of a resource.
Stable solution	Solution where neither player in a game benefits from changing from a play-safe strategy.
State	Node of a dynamic programming network.
Zero-sum game	Game in which the gain for one party is exactly matched by the loss for the other.

Summary of algorithms

Problem	Name of algorithm
Matching	Matching Augmentation
Allocation	Hungarian
Maximum flow	Labelling procedure
Critical path analysis	Drawing an activity network Early time Late time
Maximising, minimising, minimax, maximin	Dynamic programming
Zero-sum games	Play-safe strategy Mixed strategy

Index

The page numbers refer to the first mention of each term, or the shaded box if there is one.